The Reputational Premium

The Reputational Premium

A THEORY OF PARTY IDENTIFICATION AND POLICY REASONING

Paul M. Sniderman

Edward H. Stiglitz

PRINCETON UNIVERSITY PRESS

PRINCETON AND OXFORD

Published by Princeton University Press, 41 William Street, Princeton, New Jersey 08540
In the United Kingdom: Princeton University Press, 6 Oxford Street, Woodstock, Oxford-
shire OX20 1TW

press.princeton.edu

Jacket Photograph: Photo © Comstock Images. Courtesy of Getty Images.

Library of Congress Cataloging-in-Publication Data

Sniderman, Paul M.
The reputational premium : a theory of party identification and policy reasoning /
Paul M. Sniderman, Edward H. Stiglitz.
  p. cm.
Includes bibliographical references and index.
ISBN-13: 978-0-691-15414-5 (cloth : alk. paper)
ISBN-10: 0-691-15414-7 (cloth : alk. paper)
ISBN-13: 978-0-691-15417-6 (pbk. : alk. paper)
ISBN-10: 0-691-15417-1 (pbk. : alk. paper)
1. Party affiliation. 2. Political parties—Public opinion. I. Stiglitz, Edward H., 1980–
II. Title.
JF2071.S65 2012
324.2—dc23   2011039796

British Library Cataloging-in-Publication Data is available

This book has been composed in Sabon Lt Std

Printed on acid-free paper. ∞

Printed in the United States of America

10 9 8 7 6 5 4 3 2 1

To

Sophie, Allie, Hannah, Samantha, and Sadie
You will not remember, but you helped, too.

Contents

Preface

THE ORIGIN OF THIS study was a three-way partnership of Robert Van Houweling, Michael Tomz, and Paul Sniderman. We conceived of and proposed to the National Science Foundation an analysis of spatial reasoning, and we collaborated on an equal basis in the first phase of the project. Tomz and Van Houweling then focused on a series of innovative experiments to assess the comparative validity of the established formal theories of spatial reasoning.[1] In contrast, Jed and I set out on a different path. Our objective: to develop a new account of party identification, melding the insights of the social psychological analysis of voting in the tradition of *The American Voter* and those of rational choice accounts of elections in the tradition of Anthony Downs, *An Economic Theory of Democracy*. We have, however, been partners throughout: in the sense that gives true meaning to the term partnership.

It has been an adventure. We thought we had made a major discovery in our very first effort. Party loyalty, not candidate positions, was the overwhelming force. Indeed, the more strongly voters identified with one or the other of the parties, the more likely they were to perceive the candidate of their party as representing their policy position—even when there was unambiguous evidence right in front of their eyes that the position of the candidate of the opposing party was closer to their own.

With that view in mind, score a victory for the social psychological perspective of *The American Voter* over the rational choice perspective of *An Economic Theory of Democracy*. Or so we first thought. But we were wrong, wrong, wrong—all the way down, as it turned out. It has taken us years of exploration and experimentation to understand what we had first misunderstood. The result is the new theory of party identification and policy reasoning that we shall present.

Without Mike Dennis at Knowledge Networks there would have been no beginning. Then from beginning to end, we have had the support of the National Science Foundation.[2] In ways large and small, Brian Hume,

[1] See, e.g., Tomz and Van Houweling (2008, 2009).

[2] This material is based upon work supported by the National Science Foundation under Grant No. 0842677. Any opinions, findings, and conclusions or recommendations

program director for political science, has provided support. Also, the Institute for Research in the Social Sciences, under its director Karen Cook and its executive director Chris Thomsen, has given us encouragement and support to navigate choppy financial waters.

Our intellectual debts threaten to swamp us, however. At a departmental book conference, specially arranged by our colleagues Simon Jackman and Gary Segura, James Adams and Lynn Vavreck gave formal reviews of the penultimate draft of the manuscript, then followed up with written memos detailing weaknesses and identifying issues in need of attention. Whether we have reached our goal is for others to judge. But we would not have spotted the path we have followed to it without Lynn and Jim's redirecting us from the one we had been following. As for their generosity of spirit, we lack the words to express our appreciation in the measure that is their due.

Our colleagues—intellectual comrades and friends might better capture the spirit of the department of political science at Stanford—have been splendid. Morris Fiorina, in particular, read and remarked on an earlier draft. Jonathan Wand has lent us help in both detailed comments and—what he must have feared—would be endless conversations. Karen Jusko, Jonathan Rodden, and Ken Schultz suffered our interruptions with grace. We always left wiser, above all, in learning that the ideas we had arrived with were treacherously vague or, on occasion, quite simply wrong.

Each project has a life history: getting across the finish line requires getting through a (sometimes) seemingly infinite bramble bush of organizational and larger professional challenges. Nothing gives us more pleasure than to turn now and thank the three colleagues who were most helpful in getting us through—or over—or around this bramble bush. Each was invaluable in their singular way. So we shall mention each in a singular style. There is Jackie Sargent. There is Eliana Vasquez. And there is Stephen Haber. Among our colleagues in the profession we have many to thank, but we would be specially remiss if we failed to mention James Alt, Jamie Druckman, Gabe Lenz, Ted Carmines, Byron Shafer, and—for encouragement beyond measure—Jim Kuklinski. Our friend and intellectual scrutinizer nonpareil, Martin Shapiro, commented extensively (and

expressed in this material are those of the authors and do not necessarily reflect the views of the National Science Foundation.

sometimes bracingly) on the next-to-last draft. One usually thanks one's editor for encouragement. Yes, our editor, Chuck Myers, was unstinting in his support. But what sets him apart as a partner to prize is his coupling of friendship with an uncompromising insistence that our work meet his rigorous standards and his candor in telling us when it falls short.

And then there are Suzie and Kendra. An addendum: The research that we report is the joint product of Jed Stiglitz and myself. Relying on (an imperfectly memorized) precedent, however, I am happy to announce that my five grandchildren—respectively, 8, 6, 3, 2, and 1 in age at the time of this writing—have agreed, in exchange for the book being dedicated to them, to take responsibility for its shortcomings.

Stanford, June 14, 2011

The Reputational Premium

CHAPTER 1

Introduction

ARGUABLY THE DEEPEST puzzle of democratic politics is how any substantial number of ordinary citizens can reason coherently about politics. Arguably, we say, because many, possibly even most, experts would deny that citizens can reason coherently about politics. They would parade you through a chamber of horrors. The first exhibit would feature surveys of political ignorance displaying classic findings of how little citizens know about political institutions and public affairs. Next would be a display of "non-attitudes," illustrating how most citizens behave as if they are choosing sides on major issues by flipping a coin. This exhibit might be followed by charts documenting the flim-flam "structure" of citizens' beliefs about politics. Having conducted this tour of research demonstrating the ignorance of citizens about politics and the inconsistencies in their political thinking, these experts would repeat that there is no puzzle about how citizens can reason coherently about politics. The fact of the matter, regrettable but undeniable, is that all too many of them have trouble tying their shoelaces, politically speaking.

Ironically, the deeper problem lies in just the opposite direction. It is the regularity in the most important judgment they make about public affairs—casting their votes—that is most troubling. Fifty years of research backs up three claims. The majority of voters see themselves as Democrats or Republicans. The majority of them gave their loyalty to one party when they were young, that is to say, before they could have developed a considered basis for their choice. And, perhaps most worrisome, the majority of them, instead of learning from the experiences of their lives, strengthen the bond of loyalty to their party. In short, the most important factor in the most important decision a citizen can make—for whom to vote—most often appears to be rooted in an unthinking loyalty to political parties.

It is the argument of this book that party loyalty is a—and perhaps *the*—basis for reasoning coherently about the realities of contemporary

American politics. If this argument appears perverse or paradoxical, we apologize. In most studies, the influence of party identification on political judgments is the centerpiece evidence sustaining the claim that citizens' decisions derive from emotion and habit rather than considerations of policy. But the appearance of perversity or paradox is just that—appearance.

The reality of American politics is not the same as it was a half century ago. It only modestly distorts the facts to say that the official Republican Party is the spokesman for an unqualified brand of conservatism, and the Democratic Party plays the same role for liberalism. American politics at the elite level has, in a word, polarized. Republican means conservative; Democrat means liberal.

During the same period of time, voters' party identifications have become aligned with the ideological outlook of their parties. The largest number of Democrat supporters identify themselves as liberal; a still larger number of Republican supporters identify themselves as conservative. A result of this process, we shall show, is that the very same commitment that used to signal unthinking loyalty, party identification, has become the basis for coherently thinking about politics for a large number of voters. And when we say "coherently," we do not have in mind a mealy-mouthed standard of coherence. On the contrary, the standard of coherence we will employ is choosing the best informed strategy to realize their policy preferences, taking account of institutional realities.

Our aim is to present a new theory of party identification. Party identification is, for the largest number of partisans, a conjunction of an ideological as well as an emotional attachment to party. Ideological reasoning, even in a rough-and-ready way, is the last thing that voters are supposed to be capable of.[1] And yet we show that, for many voters, party identification helps them accomplish just this.

Yet our story is not one of democratic triumphalism. On the contrary, we offer a cautionary lesson on the risks of citizen competence. The democratic dilemma that thoughtful researchers and public intellectuals have focused on is: how can voters identify which candidate will better

---

[1] This was a major theme of Campbell, Converse, and Miller's classic, *The American Voter*. It continues to be a recurrent theme in public opinion research. In the formulation that Kinder has regularly repeated (1998, 2003), voters are "innocent of ideology."

represent their views when they know so little about politics? This is a troubling dilemma, and it motivates, in part, our account. But this is not the most troubling aspect of democratic representation in contemporary American politics. As we show, the more profound problem confronting the American political reality is that, just because many voters follow the best strategy to realize their policy preferences all in all, public officials have great latitude in choosing the policy hand that they want to play.

OUR STORY

The specific purpose of this study is to propose a new theory of party identification—a reputational theory of party identification. We recognize that, if we were circulating an investment prospectus, we would face skeptical investors. The study of party identification has been the most exhaustively tilled row in the study of voting. What can be gained by plowing it yet one more time?

A healthy supply—or should one say, a surfeit—of theories of party identification is already on the shelf. There is the canonical theory of *The American Voter*.[2] There also is the retrospective theory of party identification,[3] the reference group theory of party identification,[4] the performance/valence theory of party identification,[5] as well as the group identity theory of party identification,[6] to cite the most familiar names on the roster. Are we then about to tell you that all of this "conventional wisdom" is wrong?

Not at all. On the contrary, we are going to present a good deal of evidence in favor of the longest-established theory of party identification.

[2] Campbell, Converse, Miller, and Stokes (1960). For contemporary analyses of American politics centered on the canonical interpretation of party identification, see Miller and Shanks (1996) and Lewis-Beck, Jacoby, Norpoth, and Weisburg (2008). For a deeply thought through review of fairly recent research on party identification, see Johnston (2006). For a focused review of theory and research on party identification conceptualized in terms of social identity, see Bartle and Belluci (2009).

[3] Fiorina (1981).

[4] Jacoby (1988).

[5] Clarke, Sanders, Stewart, and Whiteley (2005); also see Clarke, Sanders, Stewart, and Whiteley (2009).

[6] Green, Palmquist, and Schickler (2002).

For that matter, we do not doubt that the standard measure of partisanship has a retrospective component.[7] And there are important points of similarity between the theory that we are proposing and its conceptual next of kin, notably, reference group theory and social identity theories of party identification. Why, then, propose yet another theory of party identification?

Borrowing a familiar adage, we might answer that every generation gets the theory of party identification that it deserves. The ideological clash of the Republican and Democratic parties is the engine driving contemporary American politics, and a theory of party identification that encompasses ideas as well as feelings would seem suited to the time. That is one reason to present another theory. But there is another.

A theoretical stalemate has taken place in the analysis of voting. On the one side, there is Anthony Downs' classic narrative in *An Economic Theory of Democracy*. In this story, competing candidates locate themselves on a policy dimension with an eye to winning voters' support—hence the characterization of this approach as spatial. Voters maximize their wellbeing by choosing the candidate whose policy views are closer to theirs—hence also the characterization of this approach as rational choice. On the other side, there is Angus Campbell, Philip Converse, Warren Miller, and Donald Stokes' classic portrait of citizens in *The American Voter*. In this portrayal, voters are creatures of habit and emotion. Longstanding loyalties and beliefs—above all, their identification with a political party—are the principal determinants, of their electoral behavior—hence the characterization of this approach as behavioral.

The spatial and behavioral approaches seem opposed at every salient point. The first is economic in orientation; the second is social psychological. The first focuses on choices centered on the policy positions of competing candidates, abstracting from any sense of loyalty or personal history. The second centers on the motivations of voters, the most fundamental of which is loyalties to a party that they acquired early in life and have maintained throughout it. The first argues that citizens extract significant value from their limited political information. The second makes much of the meagerness of political knowledge that ordinary citizens possess, questioning people's suitability as competent agents in a de-

---

[7] Which is not the same thing as equating party identification with retrospective judgments.

mocracy. The first is a template of rational choice; the second is taken as shorthand for vote choices made out of emotion and habit, with minimal if any consideration of policy. In the language of the trade, the first approach is spatial, since its aim is to give an account of how voters should and/or do vote as a function of candidates' locations in a policy space—*and* of where candidates strategically locate themselves in this space as a function of voters' policy preferences. The second approach has been awarded the sobriquet of behavioral, as it centers on arguably irreducible attributes of human behavior, such as emotion, that cannot be readily captured in a rational choice theory.

Initially, the behavioral approach took the lead as studies of the beliefs and biases of ordinary citizens surged in popularity thanks to the introduction of public opinion surveys. Subsequently, the spatial approach overtook the behavioral one (in our judgment) because of its capacity to provide a simple, parsimonious theory of candidate positioning.

All the same, competition has remained intense, and for a generation, the behavioral and spatial approaches worked at cross-purposes. The clash of perspectives remains, but as time has passed, they have settled down into (mostly) peaceful co-existence. Indeed, some proponents of one approach break bread with proponents of the other.[8] It is our aim to join them.

A Reputational Theory of Party Identification

In Downs' canonical formulation of spatial analysis, voters choose the party whose position is closer to theirs—however close or far that may be. In most subsequent variations of Downs' theory, however, the spatial analysis is candidate-centered—the voters ask: which *candidate* is closer to my preferred policy?[9] Our approach similarly presumes that voters make policy-based choices. But its distinctive claim is that (many) voters

[8] Showcase examples are the pioneering studies of Adams, Merrill, and Grofman (2005) and of Tomz and Van Houweling (2008). For other noteworthy examples of inclusive perspectives, see Clarke, Sanders, Stewart, and Whiteley (2005, 2009).

[9] Note that Downs himself was concerned with the positioning of parties in a parliamentary-type system. Subsequent scholars, applying his theory to the U.S. system, have largely confined attention to competition between candidates. In any event, in either the original Downsian analysis or in subsequent neo-Downsian analyses, the focus is on either parties or candidates—but not both.

take account of two, not one, sources of policy positions. One source is the policy positions of candidates, as in most spatial reasoning studies. The other is the policy reputations of the political parties under whose banner candidates run. Simply put, our account of spatial reasoning is party-centered as well as candidate-centered.

Our starting point, then, is a simple intuition: that political parties are a source of relevant policy information to ground choices between candidates. This intuition surely has sufficient plausibility to justify exploration. A generosity of spirit has been required to credit the ordinary citizen with the information and interest to make the endless list of comparisons of candidates' policy positions in a political system in which so many candidates compete for so many public offices. As compared to the galaxy of candidates and the positions they take, the policy reputations of the parties are easier to grasp; more stable over time; certainly more distinct at this moment in time; and, most importantly, able to integrate the free-ranging miscellany of policies salient at the moment into coherent political outlooks—and are accordingly effective predictors of policy outcomes all in all.

Our aim is to work out what this simple intuition that political parties are a source of policy information entails: Which voters make party-centered choices? How, exactly, do they combine candidate- and party-centered policy information? What electoral incentives do party-centered choices offer to candidates? And what are the implications of these incentives for the logic of electoral competition and a theory of democratic representation?

Answering these and other questions is the task of the chapters that follow. Here we want to call attention to two centerpiece concepts of our account. The first concept is a reputational premium.

It is accepted that the more strongly voters identify with a party, the more likely they are to support a candidate of their party independent of his policy positions. It is similarly accepted that they do so out of loyalty and habit, so much so that a vote based on party identification has become synonymous with a vote based on an emotional attachment to the party rather than a judgment about its policies. It is our claim that a large number of party identifiers now also support their parties' candidates because the candidates' policy positions reflect their party's policy positions. So far as this is so, it follows that the more strongly they identify with their party, the more likely they are to support the candidate of their party.

This extra measure of support is in addition to the support that these partisans would give because of their emotional attachment to their party. This extra measure of support also is in addition to the support that they would give a candidate of their party because of the candidate's own policy positions. And which voters provide this extra support? Party identifiers who share the outlook of their party and understand the ideological logic of the party system. They need not have a philosophy of politics. Even well-informed voters are not all that well informed. But they have a good sense of their broad outlook on politics. And they have a good sense of their parties' outlooks, too. So we refer to them as *programmatic partisans*, supporting as they do the programs of their parties, and the extra measure of support that they provide as a reputational premium.

Candidates of a party earn a reputational premium, we contend, if they take a position consistent with the programmatic outlook of their party. The crux of the matter, obviously enough, is the precise meaning of the relationship, "consistent with." This phrase suggests a variety of possible meanings. Perhaps the most obvious is this: a Democratic candidate who takes a liberal position has taken a position consistent with the programmatic outlook of the Democratic Party, just as a Republican candidate who takes a conservative position has taken a position consistent with the programmatic outlook of the Republican Party. In contrast, we shall argue for a less obvious meaning of "consistent with," on the paradoxical ground that this other meaning is more obvious, in the sense of more readily and reliably noticeable, in the tumult of electoral competition. We shall state this other meaning now and make the case for it later.

In the American party system, the candidates have taken positions consistent with the policy outlook of their party if, but only if, they have lined up vis-à-vis one another on the fundamental left-right dimension in American politics in the same order that their respective parties line up vis-à-vis one another.

We call this rule of judgment the Order Rule. It is our claim that programmatic partisans treat the Order Rule as both a necessary and sufficient condition for awarding a reputational premium to candidates of their party. Accordingly, it is a primary objective of our study to test the validity of the Order Rule, both in its own right and as compared to alternative rules that voters could quite plausibly employ.

The theory we are proposing has strict limits. It is limited, for example, in the voters it applies to—it has nothing to say about independents, most obviously. It is limited as well in the political eras to which it is most applicable, gaining traction the more polarized and cohesive the parties-in-government, losing it the more moderate and diverse they are. And it is limited as a theory of candidate positioning, specifying the range of positions that party candidates may take and collect a reputational premium, but not the reasons why they take the particular position that they do within this range.

We do not underline that our theory has limits out of modesty or defensiveness. To be blunt about it, a theory should get high grades just so far as it specifies under what conditions the variables it asserts are related are in fact related and under what conditions they are not related. The principal thrust of our reasoning and testing accordingly is to specify both the conditions that voters must meet to pay a reputational premium and the conditions that the candidates must satisfy in order to collect it.

Citizen Competence

Just so far as the theory and hypotheses that we will set out are valid, we will have identified conditions under which voters do what they have long been supposed to be incapable of doing—namely, making ideologically coherent choices over candidates and policies. To be sure, the rule that they follow to make ideologically coherent choices is not unconditionally optimal. On the contrary, we will explicitly identify a set of conditions under which citizens do best by disregarding the rule.[10] But these conditions occur only rarely in the world as it is. So the bottom line of our story is that, in the world as it is, substantial numbers of voters meet the conditions to choose the alternative on offer most likely to produce their

---

[10] There are two. The first is a failure of a Democratic partisan who knows and shares the outlook of his party to pay a reputational premium when confronted with a choice between a liberal Democratic candidate and an even more liberal Republican candidate. The second is the mirror image choice for a Republican partisan who knows and shares the outlook of his party. In a political era in which party elites are ideologically polarized, these two choice situations approach the breathtakingly hypothetical.

policy preferences all in all. And not only are they capable of doing this. We shall show that they actually do it.

This is the core of the story that we shall tell. It is a "good news" story about citizen competence, one might suppose. But it is not, to say the least, an unqualified good news story. One reason is the inherent contestability of what counts as a well-cast vote. For many students of politics, the standard of a well-cast vote is the choice of the alternative that maximizes their economic self-interest. What can we say? In politics, examples come readily to mind of when voters would have been better off materially if they had chosen one alternative rather than another. Indeed, the standard method of showing how ill-advisedly citizens vote is to present examples of people favoring, say, a tax policy that goes against their interests or holding incumbents responsible for shark attacks that ruined the summer business season.[11]

Of course, even if clear-cut choices are the rule rather than the exception, who sets the standard of what matters? Economic interest matters, to be sure. But many voters have other interests as well: ideals about how a democratic society should work, to name a prominent one. And, exceptional circumstances aside, who is entitled to pass judgment on what should matter to voters.[12]

It is their convictions, their deepest beliefs about what government should aim to achieve and how they should attempt to achieve it, that concern us. It has become a habit of thought among researchers of public opinion and voting that things go wrong at bottom because of voters' ignorance about politics. Or, if not their ignorance, their gullibility, or, if not their gullibility and ignorance, their susceptibility to emotional appeals. It

[11] We pause only to note that some of the literature examining the influence of random events on retrospective voting appears off to us. Contrary to the suggestion of some of these papers, it is quite sensible, indeed rational, for voters to hold politicians accountable for events not entirely in their control. At root, this intuition follows from the fact that voters often cannot readily determine what is a random event and what is within the control of the politician; in this information-poor environment, it is often in the voters' best interest to punish politicians for any negative outcome in the world, whether or not the politician influenced the outcome. For an early and influential paper on this topic, see Ferejohn (1986). Empirically, the key is to identify events not only that the politician does not have influence over, but (a) that he could not possibly have influence over, and (b) that voters know he could not possibly have influence over. The examples often used in this strand of the literature, such as shark attacks, also raise questions of representativeness.

[12] We encourage readers to consult Parfit (2011a, 2011b) for an immersive experience not of the indeterminacy but of the difficulty in determining what matters.

is a mistake to underestimate the roles of stupidity and selective interpretation in human affairs, we agree. But to concentrate only on the limits of human reasoning is a mistake, too. It is the argument of this study that biases in the democratic representation follow not only because some voters are politically ignorant, but for just the opposite reason: because other voters do understand the politics of their time, above all the ideological logic of the party system. This, we readily admit, is a non-standard position, and our burden in the following chapters is to convince you of its merit.

Research Strategy

Our strategy is to rely on randomized experiments. Dean Lacy and Philip Paolino (2010) have done pioneering work introducing this strategy in the study of spatial reasoning.[13] In a particularly noteworthy study, they placed their subjects in as realistic a setting as their imaginative minds could conceive to evaluate two competing conceptions of spatial reasoning. We are pleased to be following their intellectual lead, albeit by employing just the opposite strategy. We place subjects in a highly artificial situation, as you will see. The merit of their design strategy is obvious.[14] They stake a strong claim to external validity. In contrast, it is not obvious that our design strategy has any claim to external validity. How then can

[13] It may sound odd to characterize so recently published an article as pioneering. It was in our hands—and our minds—years earlier, as a conference paper in circulation. We wish to give Lacy and Paolino the full measure of credit they deserve.

[14] Since we have not hesitated to praise Lacy and Paolino's design for its realism and to flay our design for its lack of it, perhaps we may be forgiven for remarking that the strength of a naturalistic design like Lacy and Paolino's does impose some inferential costs. Respondents must infer spatial positions of candidates from nonspatial materials. But test materials have not been, and possibly cannot be, standardized and validated. Each set of newspaper stories or interviews is custom-created, study-by-study, as circumstances and hypotheses change. The gain in external validity of a naturalistic approach is thus a threat to internal validity. For example, Lacy and Paolino note that the moderate Democrat typically was seen as more liberal than the liberal Democrat "on issues of the economy, the environment, and education" (p. 6). What is more, the moderate Republican was seen to be on the liberal side (slightly) on gun control, the economy, health care, and education (p. 7). Are these violations of transitivity and directionality features of spatial reasoning in realistic contexts? Or are they unintended by-products of the use of imperfect study-specific test materials? The latter, as it seems to us, is more likely than the former, but based on the evidence at hand, it is not possible to tell whether it is the one or the other.

we claim that the results of our experiments reveal the choices that voters make and the processes by which they make them in the real world?

Our answer is that our experiments measure what they are supposed to measure thanks to—not in spite of—their artificiality. Our centerpiece hypothesis is that substantial numbers of voters place a high reliance on the policy reputations of the parties when choosing between candidates. What is the strongest test possible of this hypothesis? To place respondents in an optimal situation to make candidate-centered choices, yet observe voters making party-centered spatial choices anyway.

Our baseline experiments accordingly are designed to present our respondents with all the information necessary to make a candidate-centered choice—and no more. Moreover, we have deliberately made the information about candidates' policy positions unambiguous, immediately intelligible, and highly salient. The design of our experiments also insures that they receive no information about personal characteristics of the candidates—their race, gender, previous experiences in politics—that might induce them to make a choice between the candidates on some basis other than their policy positions. And in one crucial test, respondents receive no information about the parties under whose banner the candidates are running. In short, we stack the deck in favor of a candidate-centered model of spatial reasoning. If our experiments show that they nonetheless strongly rely on the policy reputations of the parties in choosing between competing candidates even in this extreme situation, we have presented the strongest evidence possible that they do so in the real world—in a world, that is, where the party affiliation of the candidates often is the only information that they have to work with.

That, at any rate, is our argument.

CHAPTER 2

A Reputational Theory of Party Identification and Policy Reasoning

IN THIS CHAPTER, we outline a new theory of party identification and draw out its implications for a theory of spatial voting. So that all the conceptual gears and pulleys are in plain sight, we begin with the premises of our party-centered theory of spatial voting.

PREMISES

Menu Dependence

Menu dependence is our starting point. Voters do not get their free and spontaneous choice of choices. They must choose from a menu of alternatives. Some mechanisms to help voters make politically consistent choices are necessary. One mechanism, in our view the primary one, is the political party system. Hence our decision to develop a party-centered theory of voting.

Our focus is on the electoral logic of institutional coordination. Our fulcrum is the role of political parties in coordinating the alternatives on offer. The parties do so imperfectly, to be sure, and they do so in their own interests, not out of a spirit of civic beneficence. But to the degree that they organize the menu of alternatives, political parties condition both the choices made and the process of choosing them.

Two changes in the structure of American electoral politics point the way. The first is polarization at the level of party leaders. As a library of studies has demonstrated, Democratic and Republican legislators have become increasingly cohesive and extreme in their positions.[1] The second is sorting at the level of party supporters. As a growing collection

[1] See, for example, McCarty, Poole, and Rosenthal (2006).

of studies have established, Democratic and Republican identifiers have come increasingly to share the positions and outlook of their parties.[2] And with these two changes, we claim, has come a third—the growth of a programmatic form of partisanship.   **3.**

Programmatic partisans identify with their party psychologically. But they also identify with its political outlook. Two rules of spatial voting follow from their knowing and sharing the outlook of their party. First, programmatic partisans choose between competing candidates on the basis of the policy reputations of the political parties as well as the policy positions of the candidates. Under conditions we shall specify, the result is a reputational premium—extra support for a party candidate in proportion to the strength of supporters' identification with their party and its overall policy outlook. Second, candidates collect a reputational premium if, but only if, their policy position is consistent with the policy reputation of the party. We shall propose a specific spatial rule defining the relationship "consistent with." Candidates have taken a position consistent with the policy reputation of their party if they line up vis-à-vis one another in the same ideological order as their parties line up vis-à-vis one another. The Order Rule provides an exact definition of the *range* of positions that a candidate may take, and still collect a full reputational premium. This leads to a central implication of our theory: in the contemporary era of party politics, the use of the Order Rule indicates that a wide range of positions are open to candidates from both parties. We call this implication of the Order Rule the Latitude Prediction.

Reputational premiums, the Order Rule, and the Latitude Prediction, if our account is right, define party-centered spatial reasoning.

The Institutional Basis of Party-Centered Voting

Two decades ago, Morris Fiorina (1988, 1992) raised the curtain on an institutionally based account of spatial reasoning. His premise: (some) moderate voters cast their ballots based on a prediction of how the control of institutions by political parties influences policy outcomes. By splitting their tickets—voting for Party A in legislative elections, and

---

[2] Centrally, consider Levendusky (2009a).

Party B in elections for the executive, for instance—voters moderate the expected policy outcome produced by the government. The policy outcome is the view of neither Party A nor of Party B. Rather, it reflects a compromise between the two parties. Shortly afterward, Alberto Alesina and Howard Rosenthal elaborated a similar view. "[P]olicy outcomes," they contended, "are a function not only of which party holds the executive but also of the composition of the legislature."[3]

Since then, an impressive research literature has accumulated. To pick two exemplary works: via an ingenious design Lacy and Paolino (2010) demonstrate that citizens' presidential votes depend on their expectations regarding the partisan control of Congress. In a comparative framework, Orit Kedar (2009) has worked out a general and deeply thought through analysis, developing a theory of compensatory voting in which partisans "overshoot"—that is, vote for a party further from their preferences, to obtain a policy outcome closer to their preferences from the coalition government that will be assembled after the election.

This body of work testifies that it sometimes pays to vote for a party other than—or even at odds with—the party one most prefers on policy grounds. It would be an act of literary license to suggest that our goal out-of-the-gate was to contribute to this line of research. But it is pleasing to be in a position to build off of it. We share two premises with previous research: that policy outcomes often drive vote choice and that the calculus of policy outcomes is party-centered. There is a crucial difference, though. The focus of previous research has been to develop a theory of party defection. The focus of our study is to develop a theory of the institutional logic of party loyalty.

Political parties, of course, were not always part of the American scene. In Federalist Number 10, James Madison famously railed against the pernicious influence of "factions." And, true to this view, political parties did not exist when the first Congress met in 1789. But this was a short-lived condition. By the second Congress, reliable coalitions had formed, with the Jeffersonian Republicans on one side, and the Federalists on the other side.[4] Political parties arose as a direct if unintended consequence of the institutional environment established in the Constitution.

---

[3] Alesina and Rosenthal (1996), 1311.
[4] Aldrich (1995), 77.

The country is of course immensely larger and more diverse today than it was in 1787, but even then the Founding Fathers realized the profound difficulties inherent to sustaining large-scale representative democracy. If the Republic is to endure, they saw, public policy cannot swing wildly from one year to the next; one region of the country—let alone one representative—cannot hold too much influence over the course of the nation's policy. The Founding Fathers accordingly established a deliberately fractured system of federal government. Enacting a law generally requires the approval of a majority of members in both chambers of Congress and also of the president.[5] No single institution determines the nature of public policy outcomes. Instead, public policy is a joint function of the behavior of the executive and legislative branches of government.

Just as no single institution determines public policy, within Congress at least, no single elected member determines the behavior of the institution. Each chamber of Congress is a collective body. The House consists of 435 voting members; the Senate, 100 voting members. Almost since the inception of political science as a field, congressional scholars have engaged in lively disputes over how legislative control is distributed among members of Congress.[6] Arguments draw full-throated counter-arguments over whether and the extent to which the floor median, committee chairmen, and political parties influence congressional behavior. But all agree on an elementary point. Legislative control is not given to any single member.[7] Authority over the direction of public policy is thus separated across institutions and, within congressional institutions, among elected members.

It is just at this juncture that political parties enter our story. They help overcome problems of coordination and collective action generated by decentralized control of public policy.[8] They organize the cacophony of interests within and across institutions. They also provide a framework for the electoral all-in-all judgments that voters must make. As

---

[5] Of course, Congress can also override a presidential veto with a supermajority vote.

[6] Prominently, see Cox and McCubbins (1993, 2005, 2006) and Krehbiel (1998).

[7] Even the "party boss" type theories—in which the majority party leader holds disproportionate influence over policy—generally require that the leader has at least tacit approval from the majority of members within the party caucus. In this sense, even the most atomistic understanding of congressional organization in fact recognizes the fundamentally decentralized nature of power in the institution.

[8] See Aldrich (1995); Cox and McCubbins (2005, 2006).

John Aldrich argues in his seminal theory of the origins of political parties, "government policy is determined by the collective actions of many individual office-holders. No one person either can or should be held accountable for actions taken in the House, Senate, and president together. The political party as a collective enterprise, organizing competition for the full range of offices, provides the only means for holding elected officials responsible for what they do collectively."[9]

Our concern is not with legislators but with voters who put them in or take them out of office. But understanding how voters choose between alternatives requires exploring how parties organize the alternatives on offer. We stress three characteristics of a party-organized choice set.

Characteristics of Choice Sets in Politics

In our view, three party-connected features of the menu of alternatives on offer hold special significance: (1) the low dimensionality of policy spaces; (2) the problem of rational ignorance; and (3) top-down politics.

Policy Coordination and Low Dimensionality

Policy choices call out to be made; and many of them must be made, in the strictest sense of the word "must," for not making a choice counts as making a choice. What is more, the range of policy choices is extraordinary. So, too, is their diversity. Were each choice independent of every other—or even of many others—no voter or legislator could make them coherently. Hence the pivotal role of political parties in coordinating policy alternatives.

In the language of the trade, political parties bundle policies.[10] The policies in a bundle tend to cover the same ground substantively. The process of bundling them together brings out their similarities. Political parties are imperfect coordinators. Issues involving foreign trade and immigration, for example, famously divide parties internally. It is for this reason that elections rarely focus on these issues, at least at the national level.

[9] Aldrich (1995), 3.
[10] To our knowledge, the first to introduce the metaphor of policy bundling were Carmines and Stimson (1989).

Indeed, if these issues enter an election, it often arises from the efforts of a party out of power to divide a ruling coalition. Or, as in the 2010 elections, insurgents raise the issues to challenge established co-partisans.[11] The key point, however, is that, for most issues—particularly domestic issues—political parties effectively organize issues into policy bundles.

⌐The result of policy bundling is to create a low-dimensional policy space—indeed, for long stretches, effectively a one- (or a one and a half) dimensional policy space.[12]⌐ Historically, one dimension in particular has dominated policy competition between the Democratic and Republican parties. Since at least the 1890s, the Democratic Party has been the party of social welfare liberalism. In contrast, the Republican Party has been the party of economic conservatism. It is thus no accident that the Democrats generally push for increases in social spending and increases in environmental protections. Similarly, it is no accident that the Republicans generally push for privatized responses to policy problems ranging from health care to social security.

The coordination of policies has a dynamic aspect, we want to emphasize. The Democratic Party has been to the left of the Republican Party on the primary left-right dimension since the mid-nineteenth century.[13] But how far the two parties differ itself differs. Sometimes, they are farther apart; sometimes closer together.[14] As fundamentally, when new issues come to the fore, the parties work to keep the policy space low-dimensional. But these new issues provide new opportunities for ambitious politicians. And with new issues come successful newcomers.

James Stimson has provided a sketch of the organizational incentives for accommodation. The newcomers' success poses a strategic choice for fellow party activists and candidates. Should they welcome them because they increase the party's strength all in all? Or fight them because they are committed to controversial policies with uncertain enduring electoral

[11] The most obvious example of such an insurgent challenge is J. D. Hayworth's campaign against John McCain. But immigration is part of the more general insurgent campaign within the Republican Party. For example, nearly 90 percent of Tea Party supporters, the dominant insurgent organization in the 2010 election, approve of the controversial Arizona anti-immigration law. (http://seattletimes.nwsource.com/html/politicsnorthwest/2012005031_new_poll_looks_at_tea_party_vi.html.)

[12] Poole and Rosenthal (1997).

[13] Ansolabehere, Snyder, and Stewart (2001).

[14] See Ansolabehere et al. (2001), which has been an invaluable guide for us. The classic study is Poole and Rosenthal (1997).

value? If the old-timers are neutral on the new controversial issues (e.g., pro-life versus pro-choice), whether on personal grounds or for constituency considerations, accommodation is easy. But if they have committed themselves to an opposing position (e.g., pro-choice), they do not have an easy option. Flip-flopping is costly, so holding out often is their best play.[15] Still, if the new issues prove of enduring electoral value, the position of holdouts in a party becomes more precarious over time. Defecting to the other party rarely is an attractive option. They may be in-step on an issue or two, but in an era of polarized parties, they are all too likely be out-of-step with the other party's long-established policy agenda. So holdouts tend to stay put until time itself, in the form of cohort replacement, decides the outcome. The holdouts retire from office or die in it. Their successors are attracted to the party in part because of its stands on the live issues. So consensus again becomes a hallmark of the party.

This is an ideal typical sketch, it is true. But it gets the most important thing right—the role of the party in organizing a menu of alternatives into coherent competing ideological rivals.

Policy Reputations and Rational Ignorance

Ordinary citizens have a limited demand for information about politics, to say the least. This is rational, Downs argued, because the costs of citizens acquiring information outweigh the benefits of possessing it.[16] As he and others have added, however, citizens pick up useful political information by other routes and for other reasons. Many motives and means for ordinary citizens to acquire such information about politics have been enumerated. Accidental exposure is one suggestion. Being a fan of politics is another. Acquiring information as a Collector's Item is yet another. Feeling a duty to be informed, still another.[17] And there are yet more variations of this grand theme of democratic politics' dependence on serendipity.

---

[15] See Tomz and Van Houweling (2009) for an exemplary analysis.

[16] If the cost of acquiring knowledge to vote intelligently is greater than zero, it does not pay to acquire it any more than it pays to turn out and vote. See Hardin (2009), especially chapter 3, for a characteristically lucid discussion.

[17] We have hijacked this list from Fiorina (1990), who provides the clearest and deepest discussion of the (possible) relationships between information and rationality of which we are aware.

The length of the list is proof of the ingenuity of theorists—also, perhaps, a sign of their being in a tight spot. The difficulty lies less in the theory and more in the limits of an exclusively demand-side theory of political knowledge. Curiosity, citizen duty, being a fan of politics, having a museum curator's drive for shards of political knowledge, all are efforts to add muscle tone to a theory of motivation explaining why citizens might want or desire the information sufficiently to expend the effort necessary to collect it.[18] Here, however, we want to bring to the fore a supply-side approach to a theory of political knowledge. In particular, we want to concentrate on the role of political parties in providing voters with information to make coherent policy choices and the incentives to put it to use.

A wheelbarrow full of research points the way. Gary Cox and Matthew McCubbins (1993, 2005) and John Aldrich (1995) were among the first to bring out the role of political parties as brand names in politics. James Snyder and Michael Ting (2002) have helpfully elaborated an informational rationale for political parties as brand names. They demonstrate that party labels are useful to both candidates and voters "because they provide low-cost information about the preferences of groups of candidates."[19] The voters benefit from the party label because they learn a great deal about the candidate's views from their party affiliation; the candidates benefit from the label because it allows them to communicate their preferences to the electorate without the costs of directly advertising their policy positions.

And what is the information that party labels convey? In Snyder and Ting's account, they "carry relatively precise meanings. Democratic candidates tend to be liberal, and Republicans tend to be conservative."[20] Precise would not be precisely the word that we would choose, considering the fluidity of policies defining a liberal or conservative outlook over

---

[18] Perhaps oddly, in view of this miscellany of motives, we believe that there is more to be said on a demand-side theory of knowledge. For our part, we would focus on people's inherent—and we would suggest, rational—desire to understand the world around us. And, for many, that includes politics. The issues and political personalities and causes of the day are significant. They matter to them. They speak to the meaning of their lives; to their sense of what is right and important and worthy of support—or opposition; to their desire to understand the time in which they live; to live lives that go beyond the humdrum; to have a sense of participating in an activity or cause that others recognize is deeply important.

[19] Snyder and Ting (2002), 91.

[20] Ibid.

time. "Wall-to-wall" rather than precise would be our nominee. Just so far as policy choices tend to be low- or even one-dimensional, the policy reputations of the parties cover the gamut of issues in play at a particular moment in time.

The wall-to-wall policy reputations of the parties provide a key to a puzzle in the study of public opinion. It has long been the consensus that ordinary citizens pay only intermittent attention to public affairs. It follows, as Tuesday follows Monday, that they tend to have relatively little knowledge of politics.[21] Even voters who are well-informed compared to fellow voters are, by any reasonable standard, not all that well-informed. But all the same, substantial members of the public tend to take consistently liberal or conservative positions on broad policy agendas.[22]

How can ordinary citizens manage to be consistent policy liberals or conservatives, considering how little they know about politics? By taking advantage of parties' policy reputations, we in concert with others reply. To make consistently liberal or conservative choices, it is not necessary that a citizen be able to elaborate a theory of liberalism or conservatism. It is necessary that he know the parties' policy reputations. And citizens learn them because the parties teach them, and the parties teach them not because voters necessarily wish to learn them, but because it is to the parties' advantage to teach them. Sometimes, the Democratic Party benefits by declaring itself the party of liberalism, sometimes by condemning the Republican Party as the party of conservatism. Ditto in political reverse for the Republican Party. The result: although few citizens know a lot about politics, a lot of citizens—on the order of seven in ten currently—know that the Democratic Party is the party of the left and the Republican Party is the party of the right. Know this and you have an ideological compass—one that partisans have good reason to know and make use of. Many of them, as a result, can tread an ideologically coherent path even if they are quite incapable of giving a definition of ideology.

Candidates can and do provide policy information. But so many candidates compete for public attention, and most have so little in the way of resources. Presidential candidates aside, the media hardly lavish attention on individual candidates. If candidates do become the focus of public attention, it is more likely to be on account of their peccadilloes than their

---

[21] See Delli Carpini and Keeter (1996) for the authoritative study of political knowledge.
[22] Carmines and Stimson (1989).

political ideas. A modest public presence for individual candidates is built into the institutional cards. The American political system churns through politicians. Their political careers are brief in absolute terms, and briefer still, in terms of tenure in specific offices. Most politicians change offices every few years, some out of necessity, others out of ambition. And with each change in office they must introduce themselves to a new electorate.

It is political parties that hold the key to a supply-side theory of political knowledge, we have come to believe. The parties have been doing business for a century and a half, and they have peddled their policy wares, if not at exactly the same location, then in the same ideological neighborhood for the last half century at least. So, far from attempting to conceal what they stand for, they have invested in the billboard business. They look for the social routes that people travel in their daily lives, then post eye-catching signs to attract their attention, advertising their policy reputation or publicizing that of their competitor, depending on whether the one or the other is to their advantage.

The Rise of Programmatic Partisanship

The most dramatic change in the ideological structure of American politics in a generation has been the polarization of the parties-in-government. Beginning in the 1970s, they began to take more extreme ideological positions and to become ideologically more cohesive in the mid-1970s. They have become progressively more extreme and cohesive since.

Three research programs have pointed to connections between polarization at the level of elite politics and beliefs and preferences at the level of voters. The first highlights increases in voters' awareness of polarization at the elite level as the intensity of polarization at the elite level increased. Marc Hetherington documents with particular clarity a sharp increase in the percentage of citizens who perceive important differences between the parties and who know the ideological reputation of the parties.[23] The second line of research, conducted by Thomas Carsey, Geoffrey Layman, and their colleagues,[24] indicates that party identifiers bring

[23] Hetherington (2001), 624, figure 5.
[24] See Carsey and Layman (2006). We are indebted to their research on the structure of cleavage, above all, their analysis of conflict extension rather than displacement, and we have drawn on their work at many points in developing our own thinking.

their issue preferences into line with their parties provided that they are aware of the policy differences between the parties on the issues.[25] They recognize, all the same, that partisans also bring their positions into line with their party affiliation on issues that are less important to them and, in any case, that the relationship between party identification and policy preference surely operates in both directions.

A third research program, led by Matthew Levendusky (2009a), provides a chronological map of the alignment of Republican identifiers on the right and Democratic identifiers on the left on all the principal policy agendas—cultural issues, racial issues, and New Deal issues.[26] Levendusky also has drilled below the level of policy agendas, measuring partisan sorting on an array of individual issues, running from government services, through government aid to minorities, through abortion, through defense spending, through government assistance to minorities. Partisan consensus characterizes some issues more than others. But all in all, voters' partisanship and their policy preferences now align to a degree not present even three decades ago.

Levendusky marshals evidence that this *sorting* of the electorate on a partisan basis occurred after the polarization of the partisan elite. In addition, he exploits the power of randomized experiments. His experiments employ an ingenious pictorial design to depict degrees of polarization among Democratic and Republican congressmen.[27] In the "high polarization" screen, respondents see twice as many congressmen located at polar positions than moderate ones, none in the center, and no overlapping of preferences of Democrats and Republicans. In contrast, in the "low polarization" screen, far and away most congressmen take moderate positions; hardly any take a polar one. The tails also overlap in the low polarization condition. Some Republicans take liberal and centrist positions; some Democrats opt for conservative and centrist ones. Still, the center of grav-

---

[25] To be exact, they do so provided the issue is not exceptionally important to them; if it is, they tend to bring their party attachment into line with their policy preferences. And, to be clear, there is evidence that policy preferences can drive party identification, as Carsey and Layman acknowledge. See especially Abramowitz and Saunders (2006). For our purposes, however, the direction of the relationship between party identification and policy preferences is irrelevant. What is relevant is that the two run together.

[26] Levendusky (2009a) is the definitive study of partisan sorting. His work has provided one of the principal foundations on which we have built. On sorting at the level of policy agendas, see Levendusky (2009a), chapter 5, and figure 5.1 in particular.

[27] Levendusky (2009b).

ity of each party is clearly consistent with their policy reputations. Leven-dusky's principal finding is that the sorting of party supporters increases as the degree of policy divergence between Republicans and Democrats in Congress increases.[28]

Whether party identifiers are more likely to stand with their party because they have brought their issue preferences into line with their party attachments or the other way around remains a matter of debate. Whether the ideological sorting of partisan voters is a response to the ideological polarization of party leaders is perhaps less so. Both are important questions; both could benefit from more research. But the answers to these questions are peripheral to our project. What matters for us is that, by one or another means, the largest number of partisan voters now are in synch with the program of their party. We shall argue that the consequences of this synchronization of partisanship and policy outlook call for a new theory of party identification and spatial reasoning.

Reputational Reasoning and Candidate Positioning

Traditional and Programmatic Partisanship

The canonical concept of party identification is embedded in a larger and more finely spun web of theory and analysis than commonly acknowledged. The concept itself can be economically summarized, though. On the *American Voter* view, party identification is essentially an emotional attachment to a political party.[29] Typically, this affective attachment is acquired early in life, most commonly from one's parents but not infrequently from one's peers. Characteristically, party supporters' identification with their party increases over the course of their lives. This strengthening of the bond between partisan and party can occur for diverse reasons. It may be a product of habitual exercise in election after election. It may be a consequence of the ossification of the aging process itself. But the bond between partisan and party does not strengthen out of policy conviction. Identifying with a party is only minimally, and then

---

[28] Notice that in our surveys, we ask the respondents to identify their ideological and policy views before we reveal the positions of the candidates.

[29] This remains the conception of the "Michigan" school. See Miller and Shanks (1996).

often coincidentally, related to identifying with policies that the party stands for.[30]

We shall label party identifiers who fit the canonical conception of party identification "traditional" partisans. We use this label not in a dismissive spirit, but instead to bring out the differences among programmatic partisans. These party identifiers share the political preferences and political outlook of the party that they identify with. As important, they also understand the ideological logic of the party system; that is, they understand that the Democratic Party is the party of liberalism, the Republican Party the party of conservatism. These points of difference provide the materials for a new portrait of party identifiers. Yes, they identify with their party and their attachment has an emotional component to it. But, no, their attachment is not merely a matter of emotion. It has a policy component, too. For them, to believe in certain ideas and a certain outlook on politics is to be a Democrat; to be a Democrat is to believe in certain ideas and a certain outlook on politics. Just the same holds true for most Republicans now. For them, to believe in certain ideas and a certain outlook on politics is to be a Republican; to be a Republican is to believe in certain ideas and a certain outlook on politics. Hence our practice of referring to them as "programmatic" partisans. Programmatic partisans know and share the outlook of their party. Traditional partisans do neither.

The Reputational Premium

In the neo-Downsian framework, voters compare the candidates' policy positions to their own.[31] It is not obvious how ordinary citizens can pull this off, we cannot resist the temptation to add. A goodly number of them

[30] It is an odd, and possibly instructive, fact that published research over an extended period of time pointed to the increasing, and arguably causal, connection between issue preferences and party identification without the canonical concept itself being revised. For an excellent example of this research literature, see Niemi and Jennings (1991). For a restatement of the canonical conception of party identification, see Miller and Shanks (1996).

[31] As suggested earlier, we say neo-Downsian and not "Downsian" because Downs himself was concerned with the placement of parties in a parliamentary-type system and not candidates. In the years since his dissertation was published, scholars have commonly applied the Downsian predictions to candidates and not parties. We also want to emphasize that the labels of programmatic and traditional partisans are for convenience of exposition and presentation of some of our results. Our theoretical commitment is to differences of degree, not kind.

may have a fair idea of the position of prominent incumbents.[32] But we know of no reason to believe that citizens know most of the policy positions of most of the candidates who go head to head in elections.[33]

For programmatic partisans, it is another matter. They have internalized a coherent set of preferences. They know which party stands for which outlook. True, some issues are more centrally bound up with the policy reputations of the parties; others less so. All the same, the knowledge that the Democratic Party is the party of liberalism and the Republican Party the party of conservatism can carry voters a long way. In a polarized party system, know the party banner that a candidate is running under, and you will have a very good idea of their policy positions. Know their policy positions, and you will have a very good idea of the party whose banner they are running under.

One part of our account, then, is informational. The other part is motivational. Programmatic partisans not only know the outlook of their party. They share it. When the party wins, they win. Voting for the candidate of their party is the way to realize the program of their party. In saying this, we do not assume that programmatic partisans have any particular theory of party government. Some contemporary researchers take the position that the parties exercise influence over their members in Congress; others believe that the appearance of party influence is misleading. Programmatic partisans may hold one theory of congressional government or the other or, most likely, no theory at all. What is relevant is that it is obvious, to party supporters in synch with the contemporary party system, that the preferences of members of the same party cluster together and that the preferences of members of the opposing party cluster in the ideologically opposite direction. In this polarized environment, for party supporters who know and share the outlook of their party, it is sufficient that electing a co-partisan increases the odds of their realizing their preferences all in all.

A programmatic partisan's ties with his party are bound up with what it stands for politically. So the more strongly he identifies with his party, the more likely he is to support candidates of his party if they represent what his party stands for politically. This increased likelihood of a candidate

[32] Jessee (2009).

[33] The hitch, it is worth underlining, is not computational but informational. See Gintis (2009) on the fallacy of computational "requirements" in strategic choice.

being selected by virtue of representing the programmatic outlook of a political party, we call a "reputational premium." The size of the premium is thus proportional to the number of party supporters and the strength of their identification with their party. Critically, a reputational premium is independent both of the purely non-policy, emotional component of party identification and also of the policy distance between the voter and the candidates. The premium accrues to candidates by virtue of the party whose flag they run under because they are running under its flag.

Candidate Positioning: The Order Rule

Candidates of a party collect a reputational premium for representing the outlook of the party. We take "representing the outlook" to be synonymous with candidates taking positions. But asserting the synonymy of the two is less taking a clear step forward and more like opening the door to an avalanche of possible interpretations. What, exactly, does it mean for a candidate's position to be "consistent with" his party's policy reputation?

Ours is a negative strategy: to find fault with two possibilities that come quickest to mind. Our starting point: "consistent with" cannot be a synonym for a candidate's policy position matching the policy position of the median legislator of a party. It would be cock-eyed to suppose that liberal Democratic supporters will perceive a Democratic candidate to be at odds with their party's program because he is a bit to this or that side of his party's median legislator. Ditto for conservative Republican supporters and a Republican candidate. They will not judge a Republican candidate to have defected if he does not score a bull's-eye on the location of the median Republican legisltor. Another potential meaning of consistent with is taking a position "similar" or "close" to a party's center of gravity. But then again, how similar is similar enough? How close is close enough? The ambiguity of the concept "similar" undercuts its utility.

In the standard spatial setup, two candidates locate themselves on a left-right policy dimension. The policy orientation of the Democratic Party is, and is known to be, liberal; the outlook of the Republican Party is, and is known to be, conservative. It follows that, to be correctly aligned, the candidate of the party of the left must be to the left of the candidate of the party of the right. In a polarized party system like the contemporary American one, a Democratic candidate who has located herself to the right of his Republican opponent has put herself unmistakably at odds with the Democratic Party. Likewise for a Republican candidate who has decided to take a more liberal position than the representative of the party of liberalism.

⌐The rule then is: candidates running under the parties' banners must line up vis-à-vis one another on the left-right policy dimension in the same order as the parties line up vis-à-vis one another. We call this the Order Rule.⌐ On our account, candidates who satisfy the Order Rule receive a reputational premium: an increased probability of being picked as partisans' preferred candidate on the basis of a combination of their party affiliation and policy orientation.

Figure 2.1 identifies the positions that a Democratic candidate may and may not adopt to collect a reputational premium.[34]

Consider first D_3. He has located himself to the right of the Republican candidate. He accordingly forfeits any reputational premium, obviously enough. The choices of D_1 and D_2 are more interesting. Both represent atypical cases: D_1 because he has taken an extremely liberal stand even for a very liberal party; D_2 because he has taken a conservative position, to the right of the midpoint M, even though he represents the liberal party. Yet, the positions of both satisfy the Order Rule. Both adopt positions to the left of the candidate of the party of the right. It follows, on our theory, that both D_1 and D_2 should collect a reputational premium; and what is more, D_2 should profit as handsomely as D_1, even though he crossed over the center point. Indeed, on our account, any Democratic candidate who locates to the left of his Republican opponent likewise pockets the full reputational premium.⌐So far as the positions that competing candidates choose, we maintain that satisfying the Order Rule is a sufficient as well as necessary condition for collecting a reputational premium.⌐

We recognize that our claim does not fit standard approaches to voter behavior, and we shall make plain that it is at odds also with some major

---

[34] Figure 2.1 does not address support they can win on other grounds—by best representing the position of an individual voter, for example, or by generating an appeal that goes beyond party and wins the support of political independents and, possibly, some weakly attached to the other party.

Figure 2.1: The Order Rule and the Reputational Premium

theories of spatial reasoning. Then again, we claim that falsifiability is not the least virtue of our theory.

The Latitude Prediction

According to our account, candidates need only line up in the same ideological order vis-à-vis one another as their parties line up vis-à-vis one another, and they will collect a full reputational premium. What follows if our reasoning is valid? ⌐Candidates enjoy wide latitude in terms of the positions that they may adopt, not only without suffering a penalty but still enjoying a reward. We call this the Latitude Prediction.⌐

The first thing to say about this prediction is that there are good grounds for arguing that it is false. Consider an objection at the head of the queue.

In all versions of spatial theory, candidates take positions on a policy dimension running from left to right. According to Directional Theory, voters first determine whether a candidate is on the same side of the issue they are, rewarding them if they are, punishing them if they are not. Any policy position to the left of the center point is liberal; any policy position to the right is conservative. This categorical conception of left and right fits the way that political analysts think of politics when they pronounce that a politician as "on the left" or "on the right." The first objection to the Latitude Prediction then is that it ignores directional logic. Liberal Democratic supporters do not regard a Democratic candidate who crosses over the center point as a representative of the liberal outlook of the Democratic Party.

Moreover, proponents of Directional Theory assert that a candidate increases his policy appeal by taking up a position nearer the pole than the center point of a policy dimension.[35] The intuition is that by taking a

---

[35] Directional theorists add the rider that the position should not be so near the pole as to be "extreme." There is, in their view, "a region of acceptability." See Rabinowitz and Macdonald (1989).

more marked, less moderate position, a candidate signals his commitment to the policy. So far as the extremity of the position is an indicator of the strength of his commitment to a policy, then (again to take the example of a Democratic candidate) as the candidate moves away from the left pole, the size of a reputational premium will decrease, going to zero as the candidate takes a centrist position on the policy dimension.

This objection to our account has merit. Why then do we stand by the latitude prediction? We have several reasons, but our principal one is that the on-the-shelf criticisms are exclusively candidate-centered.[36] It is an argument about support that candidates receive by virtue of their policy positions and for no other policy consideration. By contrast, the latitude prediction is predicated on the bonus that candidates can collect from their party's supporters who know and share their party's policy positions.

Our theory of party identification, if correct, thus spills over into an account of spatial reasoning. The more strongly partisans identify with their party, the more likely they are to support the candidates of their party—that is the result that *The American Voter* discovered and every subsequent study of American politics has replicated. Our interest is a policy-based partisan multiplier effect, generated by an attachment to the party's programmatic outlook.

The question then is, under what conditions will this special activation of party identification occur? It is tied to the outlook of the party, we have argued. It follows, first, that knowing the policy reputations of the parties and, second, that sharing the outlook of one's own party represent two central conditions for activation of the multiplier effect of party identification. The third condition has to do with the positions that competing candidates adopt relative to one another. It is true that the parties do not have fixed positions. The Democratic Party sometimes is farther to the

---

[36] Another reason, discussed below, is that this directional account relies on an abstract conceptualization of the policy space that many voters likely do not possess. In the directional account, that is, the voter must observe the candidate location and declare the position as "left" or "right," in some absolute sense. Although this exercise comes easily to political analysts, it actually demands of the voter a fairly abstract understanding of the policy space. What is a "left" policy, precisely? Even if the candidate's position is perfectly clear, how does the voter determine if the policy is, in some absolute sense, a "leftist" or "rightist" policy? Notice that the question of which of two candidates is *relatively* right demands far less of the voter. We return to this difference below.

left, sometimes closer to the center, sometimes more cohesive, sometimes more disparate. The same holds for the Republican Party. What are fixed, though, are the relative positions of the parties. The bundles of goods and policies of the Democratic Party fall to the left of the wares of the Republican Party. Hence the Democratic candidate must be lined up to the left of the Republican candidate, for the candidates' positions to be consistent with the policy reputations of the parties. To ask for more is to mistake the nature of party reputations. For the purposes of electoral choice, they are not defined in terms of an absolute ideological standard. They are defined relative to one another.

Reputational Choices and Spatial "Errors"

According to our theory, there are two reasons why a programmatic partisan may judge a candidate of his party to represent his policy preferences. One is because the candidate's position is closer to his. The other is because the outlook of the candidate's party is closer to his. Just so far as a party system is polarized at the level of party leaders and sorted at the level of party supporters, the two reasons overlap. Democratic identifiers are liberal, albeit mostly only moderately so; Democratic candidates are liberal, too, though generally markedly. Similarly, Republican identifiers are conservative, albeit mostly only moderately so; Republican candidates are conservative, too, though generally markedly. Typically, then, Democratic and Republican voters are presented with a choice between a (very) liberal Democratic candidate and a (very) conservative Republican candidate. Both have an easy choice since the candidate of their party is their preferred candidate on both candidate-centered and party-centered grounds.

This may be an easy choice for voters, but it is a quandary for us. Candidate-centered theories of spatial reasoning are well established. Why drag on stage the analytical machinery of a party-centered account when we already have an account of spatial reasoning that does the job?

We could argue that the standard neo-Downsian candidate-centered approach alone puts all of us in a quandary, since its signature product, the median voter theorem, is in tension—to say the least—with the signature property of contemporary American politics, the polarization of party elites.[37] In contrast, the reputational premium—and the Latitude Prediction that follows from the conjunction of the reputational premium and the Order Rule—opens the door to polarization since the party premium accrues to candidates irrespective of the extremity of their positions.]

It is an advantage that our theory accommodates ideological polarization at the level of party leaders and (relative) moderation at the level of party supporters. It is less of an advantage than might be supposed, however. A baker's dozen of reasons already have been adduced to explain why, though the median voter theorem and the actual world appear estranged from one another to the untrained eye, all is right to the tutored eye.[38] And the next worst position to having no explanations is having too many.

Our strategy, then, is to meet the issues head-on. Our tactic is to investigate when candidate-centered and party-centered policy considerations clash.

Party-Centered versus Candidate-Centered Policy Choice

On our theory, programmatic partisans have two policy grounds, not one, from which to choose between candidates. They have the policy positions of the competing candidates. In addition, they have the political outlooks of the opposing parties. How do they choose when the two sets of policy considerations conflict?

On the one side, the candidate of the opposing party is their spatial favorite. On the other, he is a candidate of the party with an opposing policy outlook. Figure 2.2 illustrates, from the perspective of a Democratic supporter, a conflict between candidate and party-centered policy choices.[39]

To bring out the theoretical issues, we have taken dramatic license. D_v, the Democratic partisan, is a moderate liberal. He has a choice between

[37] Consider Ansolabehere, Snyder, and Stewart (2001), who provide evidence suggesting that candidates rarely converge in elections.

[38] For one of the most thoughtful and incisive discussions of necessary conditions for the validity of the Median Voter Theorem, see Grofman (2004).

[39] We only consider the case when party candidates satisfy the Order Rule, given the argument we have just made that a party's candidate loses any reputational premium if he violates the Order Rule, that is, takes a position at odds with the policy reputation of his party.

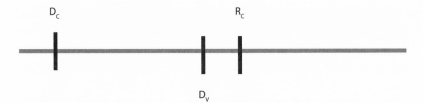

Figure 2.2: When the Other Party's Candidate Is Your Spatial Favorite

D_C, a Democratic candidate who is extremely liberal, and R_C, a Republican candidate who locates himself almost exactly at his ideal point. According to our theory, in addition to taking account of the policy positions of the two candidates, D_V takes account of the policy reputations of the two parties. The two points of reference, candidate and party, lead to different choices: the first favors R_C; the second, D_C.

What should we observe if our line of reasoning is right? Assume that D_V is a party identifier of *The American Voter* stripe. He may nevertheless have policy preferences. The fact that R_C is the spatial favorite counts in the Republican's favor, while the fact that D_C is the spatial loser counts against the Democrat. Nevertheless, if D_V is a party identifier of *The American Voter* stripe, loyalty to his party is what fundamentally matters to him. The more strongly he identifies with it, the more likely he should be to favor D_C.

Now, assume that D_V is a programmatic partisan. Policy will matter to him. The question is which policy—that of the candidate or of the party under whose banner the candidate is running. On our account, he will cast his lot with the policy of his party and, therefore, with the candidate of his party. In an era of polarization at the level of party activists and legislators, the policy reputations of the parties are well-known.[40] D_V would select R_C if all he knew or cared about were the policy positions of the candidates. But D_V identifies with his party and what it stands for. D_C, the Democratic candidate, has taken an extremely liberal position, while the voter holds only a moderately liberal position. But—and this is the vital

---

[40] In our data, on the order of seven out of ten voters know the parties' policy reputations; in the 2000 National Election Studies (NES), the corresponding figure approaches eight out of ten; in the 2004 NES, the figure stands at about three out of every four respondents. We remind in passing that "knowing the parties' policy reputations" means knowing that the Democratic Party is to the left of the Republican Party.

point—on our account, the position of D_C is consistent with the political orientation of the Democratic Party and he knows it. Voting for D_C gives him the opportunity to vote for a candidate who stands with the party that he believes in. He will choose him, then, and the more strongly that he identifies with his party, the higher the probability that he will do so. Indeed, because his identification with his party incorporates both a commitment to what it stands for and an emotional attachment, the effect of party identification should be markedly stronger for him than for a party supporter of *The American Voter* variety.

Our account, if right, is doubly ironic. First, for the largest numbers of partisans, party identification, which has been identified with an emotional habit devoid of policy content, is a force driving policy-centered choices. Second, in the Downsian scheme, preferring the candidate who is further from your position to the one who is closer is a spatial error—unequivocally and emphatically an error. Yet, it is our claim that it is the ideologically sophisticated partisans, not their politically naïve cousins, who are more likely to make this "error" in spatial reasoning. If true, this raises a provocative question. In the contemporary American party system, can a Downsian spatial error represent a voter's best chance to realize his policy preferences all in all?

CHAPTER 3

Lessons from a Sterile Downsian Environment

A PARTY-CENTERED THEORY of spatial reasoning is necessary to supplement candidate-centered theories, we have become persuaded. The strongest test of a theory is to stack the odds in favor of its rival and see if the evidence nonetheless supports it. Since a party-centered approach is the one that we shall argue for, our strategy is to stack the odds in favor of a candidate-centered choice. So we deliberately have created an experimental setting biased in favor of candidate-centered spatial reasoning, removing any reference to political parties or their programs. Our prediction is that, in spite of the absence of any reference to parties, many party supporters will nonetheless take into account the parties' policy reputations in choosing between candidates. Their doing so, absent a reference to the parties, will be the highest card one could play in support of the hypothesis that the parties' policy reputations influence their choices in the world of real politics, where the parties are among the most prominent features of the political landscape.

ISSUES OF IDENTITY

The Downsian paradigm is now an integral part of the tool kit of political scientists in all fields. Figure 3.1 illustrates the standard depiction: two candidates, A and B, position themselves on a single policy dimension with an eye to winning the support of V, the voter. But though A and B are two individuals competing for office, are they only individual candidates? In the current conditions of American politics, we claim that they are associated with parties in the minds of many—appropriately as it happens. Candidates are associated with political parties, because the parties supply the policy context that gives candidates their political identities. We recognize that that is not true of all candidates and voters. But it is true of a large, possibly even the largest, number of both of them.

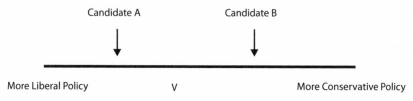

Figure 3.1: Idealized Downsian Electoral Competition

Stephen Ansolabehere, James Snyder, and Charles Stewart's ground-breaking study of candidate positioning illuminates key conceptual and empirical issues.[1] Their study details the three principal predictions of the Downsian model. (1) Candidates should converge, if not at the national level, then at the district level. (2) Candidates should be responsive to the preferences of their constituents, if not in the general election, then in the primaries. (3) Candidates have incentives to take moderate rather than extreme positions.

Ansolabehere and his colleagues find some evidence consistent with all three theoretical claims. More competitive districts tend to produce more moderate candidates. Candidates in competitive districts tend to converge, they also report, particularly when high-quality candidates are in the race. Yet, what is striking to Ansolabehere and his colleagues is not the absence of evidence in support of the Downsian model, but its weakness.

What, then, is the dominant result of their study? Examining House races from 1874 to 1996, they find that the Democrat is "to the left" of the Republican in all but two of the 1,814 races since 1874. The absolute amount of divergence between the national parties varies in a periodic fashion, they observe. Divergence was marked between the 1820s and 1930s, then decreased from the 1940s through the 1970s. Ideological polarization, though, has since returned to its historic levels. Programmatic outlooks define the identity of the national parties once again.[2] In turn, and this is the fulcrum of our account, the ideological identities of the national parties provide a context for policy-centered evaluation of positions of party candidates at all levels.[3]

[1] Ansolabehere, Snyder, and Stewart (2001).
[2] See, for example, Poole and Rosenthal (1997). See also McCarty, Poole, and Rosenthal (2006).
[3] We are indebted to Professor Lynn Vavreck for bringing out the central role of the nationalization of the political parties for our reputational theory of party identification.

A Thought Experiment: Policy Reasoning in a Sterilized Downsian Space

Since Downs, the defining rule of the voter's rationality is a voter's choice of the candidate whose policy position is closest to his. Call this the proximity rule. Here is a thought experiment to test the generality of a candidate-centered proximity rule.

In our thought experiment, we ask a nationally representative sample of citizens their position on a policy. Since we are studying spatial reasoning in our thought experiment, we would like measurement conditions to be ideal. So all respondents are provided with a computer monitor. To put them in just the right frame of mind for a study of spatial reasoning, the alternatives on offer are visually presented in a spatial format. The monitor screens thus display a policy dimension, one pole anchored by a liberal policy alternative, the other by its conservative competitor, and respondents are asked to indicate their position by locating themselves on this policy dimension.

The second step is to show them a screen depicting the positions of two candidates on the very same policy on which they themselves took a position. Everything in the second screen parallels the first. It is the same policy, described word-for-word in the same way, presented in the same spatial format—a single policy dimension anchored at each end by brief descriptions of liberal and conservative policy alternatives, again word-for-word identical with those in the first screen. The candidates are alphabetically denominated—candidate A and candidate B—and their positions are marked by arrows directed to points on the policy dimension. The positions of both candidates are randomly varied, covering all possible combinations, with the exception of ties (since a choice between them on the basis of policy would then be moot). Respondents are then asked whether candidate A or candidate B represents their position. Their choice of candidate A or B is the dependent variable in our thought experiment.

Our thought experiment mimics a thoroughly sterilized Downsian choice situation. The candidates locate themselves on a policy dimension. Their positions are not only conveyed in a spatial format. They are also unequivocal, eliminating uncertainty or ambiguity. And what respondents are not informed about counts for as much as what they are informed about. In particular, no mention is made about the candidates' backgrounds, or their previous offices or voting records, or their personal characteristics such as race or gender, or—above all—their party affiliation. So voters are told all they need to know to make a candidate-centered spatial choice. And they are told nothing that could distract them or confuse them or lead them to discount the spatial information that they receive. In these conditions, their choice between candidates on policy grounds is not merely determined. It is over-determined.

Now comes the third part of our thought experiment—the analysis of respondents' spatial choices. Imagine that we have assembled a sample of expert researchers on elections. The question we put to them is this. In these circumstances, will a voter choose between candidates A and B on the basis of policy proximity or his party identification? Without exception, they have asked us why we are asking them this question. What possible difference could it make, in this situation, whether a voter identifies with the Democratic or Republican Party? Party loyalties will count for nothing; the candidates' policy positions will count for everything, since that is all that distinguishes them.

So our colleagues thought. So we thought, too.[4] It will be all the more interesting therefore to observe the results when our thought experiment is translated into a real experiment.

THE DOWNSIAN EXPERIMENT

We begin with the Downsian paradigm experiment.[5] For this study, as for all of our subsequent studies, nationally representative samples were selected by Knowledge Networks (KN) with the interviews carried out using KN's web-based technology.[6]

The first step in the Downsian experiment is measurement of respondents' policy preferences. The test issue is government services and spending. It is the focal issue for our analysis of spatial reasoning because it taps the deepest cleavage in American electoral politics, over the responsibilities

---

[4] Van Houweling and Sniderman (2004).
[5] This section draws on van Houweling and Sniderman (2004).
[6] See appendix B for a description of the properties of data sets used in this project.

of government and the duties of citizens.[7] Measurement of preferences on the issue of government services and spending follows a general principle. Here and everywhere, we make use of standard National Election Study measures whenever we can, not because they necessarily are ideal, but rather because they are standard. Their behavior in our studies can thus be benchmarked against their performance in many other studies over many other years.

Specifically, the Downsian experiment begins with a screen presenting locations on a 7-point scale on government services and spending. The poles are anchored by brief policy descriptions. One anchoring position is that government should provide fewer services, even in areas such as health and education, to reduce spending, defined as 1 on a 7-point scale. The other anchoring position is that government should provide more services, even if it means an increase in spending, defined as 7 on the 7-point scale. Respondents are told that people take positions at all the points on the scale. Then they are asked, "Where would you place yourself on this scale?" They also are provided with the option of not expressing an opinion. So the test item includes a standard escape clause, ". . . or haven't you thought much about this?" Respondents are asked to indicate their position by clicking on a point on a scale, at the bottom of the screen, visually anchored at the two poles by short descriptions of the competing policies. Figure 3.2 reproduces the survey interface.

A miscellany of questions was inserted between the first step of the experiment, measurement of respondents' policy preferences, and the second step, presentation of candidates' policy positions. In all, twenty-nine questions intervened between measurement of respondents' policy preferences and their reactions to candidates' policy positions. The idea was not merely to separate the two judgments temporally. It was also to separate them cognitively. Asking questions about a variety of other matters, we reasoned, would divert respondents' attention from the position that they themselves had on the government services and spending item.[8] Then, having driven respondents through the equivalent of a cognitive car wash, came the test measure—choice between candidates.

[7] See, for example, Stonecash (2000); McCarty, Poole, and Rosenthal (2006); Bartels (2006).

[8] As it developed, subsequent studies indicate that this separation of measurement of respondents' preferences and presentation of candidates' positions was an unnecessary precaution. Still, better safe than sorry.

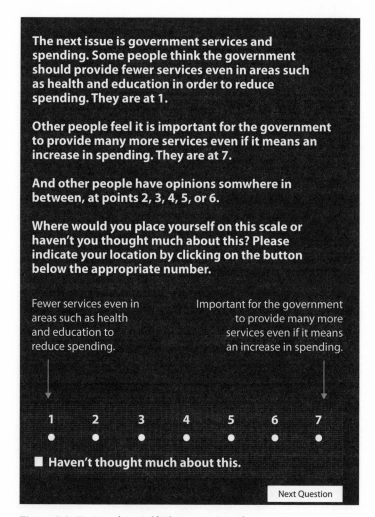

Figure 3.2: Respondent Self-Placement Interface

The screen, reproduced in Figure 3.3, shows the positions of two candidates, candidate A and candidate B, on the government services and spending item. In this particular instance, B has taken a centrist position (at 4) and A, a slightly liberal one (at 5). The visual presentation depicting the policy alternatives and the candidates' positions is exactly the same as for the assessment of the respondent's own position on the issue of government services and spending: same issue, same visual

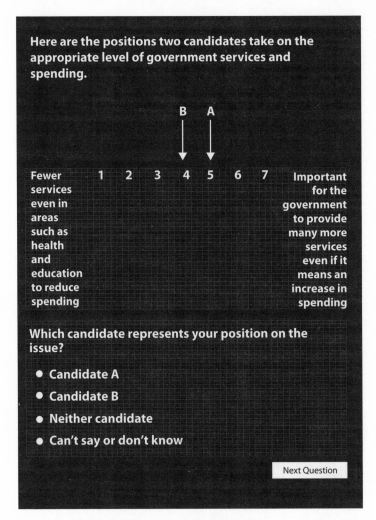

Figure 3.3: Candidate Placement Interface

format, same wording anchoring the two poles. As for the candidates, they are assigned all possible positions but for a tie. Since the assignment of candidate positions is random, it is therefore independent of the respondents' own positions on the issue, removing the inferential indeterminacies that have crippled the analysis of policy voting in standard public opinion surveys.[9]

[9] See the classic analysis of Brody and Page (1972).

Vote choice is what we are interested in, ultimately. But we lacked the confidence to begin our research program by asking about it directly. All that respondents know about the candidates is their position on one issue. Asking people to "vote" pushed the envelope on plausibility, we feared. Respondents would oblige us with an answer, we knew. But they might not take the task seriously; they might suppose that they were being asked to throw a dart, blindfolded. An alternative would have been to ask respondents which candidate's position was "closer" to theirs. But we decided that the downstream costs were unacceptable. Spatial proximity—choosing the closer candidate—is the standard decision rule. But there are other rules for making spatial choices.[10] Why start off privileging one over others? For the record, in subsequent studies we have used a variety of formulations—Which candidate would you vote for? Which candidate best represents your general outlook? The various formulations are operationally interchangeable.[11] For the Downsian experiment, we settled on a formulation that has the advantage of being direct without the disadvantage of being either implausible or leading. "Which candidate represents your position on the issue?" with respondents given the option of choosing "Candidate A," "Candidate B," "Neither," or "Don't Know."

There you have the set-up of the experiment: first, measure respondents' spatial policy preferences; then, measure their choice between candidates on the basis of their (randomly assigned) spatial policy positions. With these pieces of information, it is a trivial matter to calculate the probability of respondents picking their Downsian winner—that is, the candidate whose position is closer to theirs.

The established theory of spatial reasoning assumes that voters choose candidates based on the candidates' policy positions. A premise of the theory that we laid out in chapter 2, however, is that programmatic partisans also take account of the policy outlooks of political parties. What, we asked ourselves, would be the strongest test of our claim that spatial choices are based on the policy commitments of the parties as well as the policy positions of the candidates? Our answer: conclusive evidence that they take account of the parties' policy reputations *even when there is no reference—none at all—to the political parties*. Hence the design of the

---

[10] Adams, Merrill, and Grofman (2005) is the outstanding analysis of the interplay of the trio of spatial rules—proximity, directional, and discounting.

[11] For further evidence, see Tomz and Van Houweling (2008, 2009).

Downsian experiment: choices defined by the (fully randomized) policy positions of two anonymous and alphabetically denominated alternatives, candidate A and candidate B, in a choice situation rigged in favor of candidate-centered choices. If, even so, significant numbers also make party-centered choices, one can only imagine the power of parties shaping electoral choices in the real world in which political parties are among the most prominent parts of the political landscape.

Party and Partisanship in the Absence of Party

The question posed in our thought experiment is whether party identification, in addition to policy preferences, will influence candidate choice in the absence of any reference to the party affiliations of the candidates. Accordingly, we estimate the probit regression model of voter choice:[12]

$$\Pr(\text{Vote}_i = A) = \phi(\alpha + \beta_1 \text{PID}_i + \beta_2 A \text{ closer}_i) \qquad (3.1)$$

The first coefficient, β_1, captures the influence (if any) of party identification. The second coefficient, β_2, gauges the impact of issue proximity—the advantage that a candidate obtains in winning a voter's support because his policy position is closer than that of his competitor to the voter's. The results, presented in table 3.1, will warm the heart of every expert we asked to make a prediction about our thought experiment. The spatial proximity coefficient is obviously substantively as well as statistically significant. But the coefficient for party identification is insignificant not only substantively but also statistically. Our respondents are behaving like gimlet-eyed Downsians and not at all like party-centered reasoners.

On the theory that we have proposed, the nub of the matter is that the Democratic and Republican parties now stand for programmatic policy outlooks. Purely as a matter of fact, it is uncontroversial that the candidates of the two parties tend to land on opposite poles on a left-right

---

[12] We refer to the dependent variable as a "vote" for expository convenience; as we note above, we do not prompt respondents to "vote" over the candidates. Instead, in the experiment relevant to equation (3.1), we ask the respondent which candidate represents his position.

TABLE 3.1: Partisanship and Candidates without Party Labels

Constant	−1.06
	(0.09)
Party ID	0.03
	(0.02)
Candidate A Closer	1.57
	(0.07)
N	1487
Pseudo R-Squared	0.35

Note: Dependent variable takes a 1 if voted for candidate "A" and a 0 if voted for candidate "B."

dimension, indeed, so much so that legislative representatives of the two minimally overlap. It follows that the candidate on the left is an odds-on favorite of being a Democrat, the candidate on the right a possibly still better bet to be a Republican. It also follows that programmatic partisans should take this fact of political life into account. What does this imply about the analysis of the Downsian experiment?

In the experiment, policy positions are randomly assigned to Candidates A and B. Table 3.1 reports the results related to choosing candidate A as representing your position. But because policy positions are randomly assigned to candidates A and B, one-half of the time candidate A takes a position to the *left* of candidate B. However, the other one-half of the time, candidate A takes a position to the *right* of candidate B. If policy positions are proxies of party affiliation, a programmatic Democrat would choose candidate A half the time—when candidate A was the candidate on the left, and candidate B the other half, when candidate B was the candidate on the left. The same is true, in reverse, for a programmatic Republican. The result: no relationship between party identification and candidate choice.[13]

What, then, is necessary to begin to test the party-centered hypothesis? If taking a liberal position is a proxy for being a Democrat and taking a conservative one is a proxy for being a Republican, it is necessary to recode the candidates, so that L stands for all candidates who took the more liberal position, ignoring whether they are denominated candidate

[13] Robert Van Houweling was indispensable in this analysis.

A or B, and C for all candidates who take the more conservative position, again ignoring whether they were denominated as candidate A or B. Having done so, we estimate the following equation:

$$\Pr(\text{Vote}_i = L) = \phi(\alpha + \beta_1 \text{PID}_i + \beta_2 L \text{ closer}_i) \tag{3.2}$$

Table 3.2 presents the results of this analysis. Candidate proximity is still the dominant rule of choice.[14] But then again, it could hardly be otherwise. We have created a Downsian heaven for voters to identify their spatial favorite. The striking result in table 3.2—striking to us, certainly—is that the party identification of the respondent now matters; and it is worth remarking that it matters notwithstanding the fact that the respondents' orientation on the policy issue itself also matters.[15]

To get some sense of the substantive impact of party loyalty, figure 3.4 translates the probit coefficients into estimates of the probability that candidate preference is a function of strength of party identification, while controlling for spatial proximity of the candidates. The dotted line tracks the probability of choosing the candidate on the left, when the candidate on the left is the respondent's spatial favorite, as a function of strength of party identification; the solid line, the probability of choosing the candidate on the left, when the candidate on the right is the respondent's spatial favorite, also as a function of strength of party identification.

As figure 3.4 shows, when the candidate on the left is their spatial favorite, on the order of 85 percent of strong Democrats pick him as representing their position.[16] No mystery here, we must say. Respondents are picking their spatial favorite when they have unequivocal, readily understandable information identifying the spatial winner. Still and all, far and away most strong Democrats make the rational—that is, Downsian—choice. In contrast, strong Republicans are dimwitted Downsians. The

---

[14] Substantively, the probability of supporting the left candidate increases to 73 percent from 33 percent when the left candidate holds a closer position.

[15] In entering ideology on the right-hand side, we are "over-controlling," since political outlook is part of the phenomenon of programmatic partisans. We have nonetheless chosen to do so to guard against the possibility that the preferences of partisans at the extremes might bias the results. Results available on request.

[16] By way of warning, we want to underline that projection of effect sizes from our experimental setting to the world of actual politics is not warranted.

TABLE 3.2: Partisanship and Candidates without Party Labels

Constant	−0.1
	(0.1)
Party ID	−0.14
	(0.02)
Left Candidate Closer	1.42
	(0.08)
N	1487
Pseudo R-Squared	0.36

Note: Dependent variable takes 1 if voted for left candidate and 0 if voted for right candidate.

candidate on the left is their spatial favorite. But only 60 percent of them say that he is the candidate who better represents their position. You might say that a majority of them get it right. A more appropriate way to think of the gap between them and strong Democrats, as it seems to us, is that it is about the distance between one group getting an A+ and another a C+.

Awarding a higher grade to Democrats would be premature, though. Consider what happens when the candidate on the right is the respondent's spatial favorite. Now, the tables have turned. As figure 3.4 also shows, when the Downsian winner is the candidate on the right, approximately 80 percent of strong Republicans pick their spatial favorite, compared to about 60 percent of strong Democrats.

The two sets of results are consistent, of course. A partisan's spatial favorite may be, by inference from his policy position, the candidate of his party. Alternatively, by the same reasoning, his spatial favorite may presumptively be a candidate of the opposing party. In the first situation, both bits of policy information, the candidate's express policy position and their inferred party affiliation, are consistent; in the second, they are at odds. Democrats and Republicans are deft at handling spatial choice when policy and party point in the same direction; both are more ham-fisted when they point in opposite ones.

We have spoken in categorical terms, contrasting the responses of strong Democrats and strong Republicans in particular. In fact, the relationship between party identification and the choice of which candidate represents

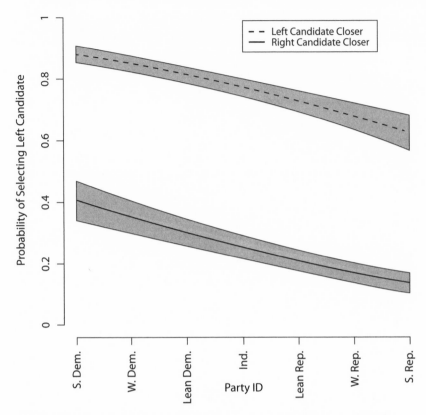

Figure 3.4: Partisanship and Candidates without Party Labels by Left-Right Position

a respondent's position is continuous: the stronger Democrats identify with the Democratic Party, the more likely they are to pick the candidate to the left even though he is not their spatial favorite; the stronger Republicans identify with the Republican Party, the more likely they are to pick the candidate to the right even though he is not their spatial favorite. Here is a *possible* illustration of a reputational premium being awarded to a candidate based on his inferred party's policy reputation, distinguished from the support a candidate receives as a result of the proximity between the candidate and the voter. The word possible deserves to be stressed, since this result is merely the beginning of a test of a reputational account of party identification.

The Policy Reputations of the Parties

Within our theory, the policy reputations of the two parties are the mechanism governing party-centered spatial reasoning.[17] In the Downsian paradigm experiment, the only information provided is about the candidates' policy positions. We presume that the parties provide a framework for evaluation of the candidate's policy positions; indeed, so immediate a framework that, among other things, some of their supporters can winkle out the party affiliation of candidates knowing only their policy positions. Our line of reasoning manifestly presumes that these supporters know the policy reputations of the parties. What sense would it make to say that partisans infer the party affiliation of candidates from the positions candidates take if they did not know the political outlooks of the parties? A test of this line of reasoning, albeit a low hurdle test, is whether there is an interaction between party identification and knowledge of the parties' policy reputations. We therefore estimate the following probit equation:

$$\Pr(\text{Vote}_i = L) = \phi(\alpha + \beta_1 \text{PID}_i + \beta_2 L \text{ closer}_i + \beta_3 \text{Reputations}_i + \beta_4 \text{PID}_i{}^* \text{Reputations}_i) \tag{3.3}$$

The first two coefficients have already been introduced. The third, β_3, is a coefficient representing knowledge of party reputations (measured in the standard NES format).[18] The interaction term, denoted by coefficient β_4, represents the caboose of the prediction equation, attached to test the hypothesis that partisans who know the outlooks of the parties are more likely to pay a reputational premium than those who do not.

Table 3.3 presents the results of the probit regression. Focusing on the coefficients on party identification (β_1) and the relevant interaction term (β_4), one can see that there is a deep interplay between partisanship and knowledge of the party's policy reputations. The influence of the former is conditional on the latter. Party identification has no impact on candidate

[17] We use the concept of mechanism in the sense that Elster has assigned it as a "frequently occurring and easily recognizable pattern" (2007, 36) providing a sense of how things work.

[18] The test of knowledge of the ideological logic of the party system is the standard NES item: "In general, thinking about the political parties in Washington, would you say that Democrats are more conservative than Republicans, or Republicans are more conservative than Democrats?"

TABLE 3.3: Partisanship and Knowledge of Party Policy Reputations

Constant	−0.35
	(0.16)
Party ID	−0.04
	(0.04)
Left Candidate Closer	1.39
	(0.08)
Knows Reputations	0.35
	(0.18)
Party ID X Knows Reputations	−0.12
	(0.05)
N	1484
Pseudo R-Squared	0.37

Note: Dependent variable takes 1 if voted for left candidate and 0 if voted for right candidate.

preference for partisans who do not know the programmatic outlooks of the parties. They do not know that Democrats are generally more liberal than Republicans, so they cannot infer that the candidate on the left is a Democrat, and party identification is therefore silenced. On the other hand, party identification manifestly has a significant impact on candidate choice for those who do.

To provide a more intelligible sense of the meaning of the results in table 3.3, figure 3.5 translates the probit coefficients into the predicted probability of picking the candidate on the left as a function of strength and direction of party identification. The left panel presents the predicted probabilities of those who do not know the policy reputations. The right panel does the same job for those who know the policy reputations of the parties.

Consider the difference in predicted probabilities, conditional on strength of party identification, depending on whether the candidate on the left (dotted line) or the candidate on the right (solid line) is the voter's spatial favorite.[19] For the group of respondents who do not know the policy reputations of the parties, in the left panel of the figure, the probability of selecting the left candidate is roughly constant across values

---

[19] We use "spatial favorite" and "Downsian winner" interchangeably. Both refer to the advantage a candidate gets by virtue of his policy position being closer to a voter's than his competitor.

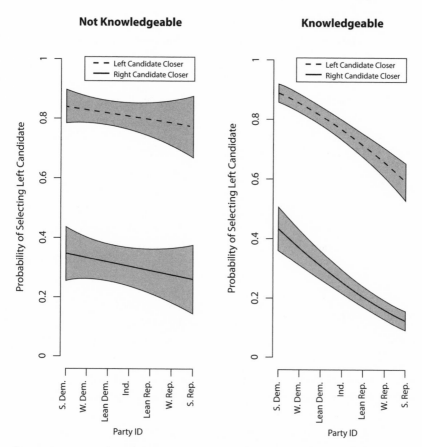

Not Knowledgeable

Knowledgeable

Figure 3.5: Party Identification and the Probability of Consistent Policy Choice by Knowledge of the Ideological Structure of the Party System

of party identification. In a word, candidate choice is unrelated to party identification for those who do not know the programmatic outlooks of the two parties.

Now consider the choices of partisans who *do* know the policy reputations of the parties, candidate choice, and party identification are manifestly tied together. Both the dotted line (candidate on the left the voter's spatial favorite) and the solid line (candidate on the right the voter's spatial favorite) slope downward, steeply, from left to right. And just as one would and should expect, more than 80 percent of strong Democrats chose the candidate on the left when he is their spatial favorite. On the other hand, approximately 40 percent of strong Democrats do the same when he is not their spatial favorite. The same is true for strong Republicans except the other way around.

What does this add up to? The canonical interpretation of party identification is a story about blind loyalty. Strong identifiers are more likely to stick than weak identifiers with the candidate of their party through thick and thin, in good times and bad, when he represents their position and when he doesn't. Figure 3.5 shows that—absent party labels—party identification promotes party loyalty—*but if and only if party identifiers know the political parties' policy reputations*. This suggests a rather different interpretation from the canonical conceptualization of party identification. Based on this figure, the more strongly partisans identify with their party, the more likely they are to use the candidates' policy positions as proxies for their party affiliations. They then decide which candidate they prefer on the basis of the imputed party affiliation, favoring him if he likely belongs to their party, opposing him if he likely belongs to the opposing party. This is a story of loyalty, all right, but hardly a story of blind loyalty. Knowing the parties' reputations is key.

This result definitely represents a passing grade on our theory's report card, but as grades go, it is not much better than a B-. One reason that it contributes only a modest amount of support for our line of reasoning is that there is another quite obvious—and obviously plausible—line of reasoning that generates the same prediction. Why assume that it is one particular bit of knowledge—knowing which is the more conservative and which the more liberal party—that is pivotal? Isn't it just as reasonable—indeed, more reasonable—to expect that what counts is political awareness and sophistication in general, not one particular bit of knowledge about the party system? After all, our measure of knowledge of parties' policy reputations is a standard component of measures of political knowledge and sophistication in general.[20] If knowledge of the parties' political outlooks is just one of a number of indicators of the latent trait of political sophistication—and there is a good deal of evidence for just this—the right story to tell may have nothing to do specifically with political parties. Instead it may be a story of political awareness and sophistication in general.

[20] Delli Carpini and Keeter (1996).

The publication style in social science is: presentation of hypotheses; description of methods; then reporting of results—all written up as if everything had gone according to plan. Regardless of whether this is a fair description of other studies, it is not an accurate description of this one. We did not derive our theory from first principles. We did not even start out with an intuition about its key components—a reputational premium and the Order Rule. We did start out with a suspicion that a body was buried. But when we dug it up, clue after clue led us away from our first suspect, *The American Voter* conception of party identification, to a reinterpretation of partisan reasoning on Downsian lines. If we are following the right trail, then knowledge of their policy reputations should be what counts, not knowledge of politics in general.

Consistent with previous research, we have assembled an Index of General Knowledge of Politics.[21] The Index comprises four questions. Two are multiple choice: Whose responsibility is it to determine if a law is constitutional or not? and, How much of a majority is required for the U.S. Senate and House to override a presidential veto? Two are true-false: John Ashcroft is the Chief Justice of the Supreme Court and Tony Blair (as he was at the time of the study) is the Prime Minister of Great Britain. Considering the brevity of the Index, its reliability is rather impressive: alpha = .71.

The question is whether knowledge of party reputations in particular or knowledge of politics in general is a key to the special activation of party identification that results in a reputational premium. We re-estimate our basic regression, this time investigating the impact of general political knowledge as well as knowledge of party reputations, plus of course the interactions of each with party identification. Accordingly, we estimate:

$$\Pr(\text{Vote}_i = L) = \phi(\alpha + \beta_1 \text{PID}_i + \beta_2 L \text{ closer}_i + \beta_3 \text{Reputations}_i + \\ \beta_4 \text{PID}_i{}^* \text{Reputations}_i + \beta_5 \text{Knowledge}_i + \beta_6 \text{PID}^* \text{Knowledge}_i) \quad (3.4)$$

All but the last two coefficients in equation (3.4) are part of a now familiar cast of characters. β_5(Knowledge) captures the direct effect of general knowledge of politics. β_6(PID*Knowledge) is the pivotal coefficient. If β_6(PID*Knowledge) is significant and β_5(PID*Reputations) is

[21] We specifically want to thank Michael Delli Carpini for recommendations on items to form our short-form Index of Political Knowledge.

not, then we know that the policy reputations of the parties play no special role in triggering party identification in making spatial choices. If it is the other way around, then we know that knowledge of the policy reputations of the parties is the crucial piece of knowledge in triggering party identification.

It is a banal truth that if people have knowledge of one aspect of politics, they are more likely to have knowledge of another. Bits of knowledge about politics accordingly tend to be treated as interchangeable. There is nothing that distinctively follows for reasoning about politics, from knowing the number of justices on the Supreme Court as opposed to knowing the number of terms that a president may serve. Both are indirect indicators of political awareness, as near in diagnostic value as makes no difference. In contrast, a reputational theory of party identification inherently assigns a special status to knowledge of the parties' programmatic outlook. Knowing that the Republican Party is the party of the right and the Democratic Party is the party of the left is the key to the policy menu of the American party system. The concept of a reputational premium posits that partisans will pay a support premium to a candidate of their party in exchange for the candidate representing the programmatic outlook of their party. If this line of reasoning is right, then knowledge of the parties' policy reputations is not just another bit of knowledge. It is a crucial piece of knowledge.

Table 3.4 puts this line of reasoning to a test. It contrasts the efficacy, in generating a reputational premium, of one bit of knowledge, namely knowledge of the programmatic orientations of the parties, against a multiple indicator measure of knowledge of politics in general. The key terms in equation (3.4), it follows, are the two interaction terms. It is logically possible, but empirically unlikely, that both may be significant. It also is logically possible, and pragmatically quite likely, that neither will be significant, since the two measures of political knowledge naturally are correlated ($r = .42$). But supposing that our measures are up to the task of distinguishing the two, the question is, Is it a specific piece of knowledge or knowledge of politics in general that triggers partisans to support the candidate of their party the more strongly that they themselves identify with their party?

The last two rows of table 3.4 provide an answer. On the one hand, the interaction between party identification and knowledge of the parties' policy reputations is significant (t-value = 2.2). On the other, the interaction between party identification and knowledge of politics in gen-

TABLE 3.4: Partisanship, General Political Knowledge, and
Knowledge of Party Policy Reputations

Constant	−0.31
	(0.23)
Party ID	0.01
	(0.06)
Left Candidate Closer	1.35
	(0.08)
Knows Reputations	0.38
	(0.19)
General Political Knowledge	−0.01
	(0.07)
Party ID X Knows Reputations	−0.11
	(0.05)
Party ID X General Knowledge	−0.02
	(0.02)
N	1482
Pseudo R-Squared	0.37

Note: Dependent variable takes 1 if voted for left candidate and 0 if voted for right candidate.

eral is not significant (t-value $= 1.3$). In short, knowledge of politics in general is not the key to a reputational premium; knowledge of the parties' programmatic outlooks is.

Replication: Reputations of the Parties versus Knowledge of Politics in General

Ours is a party-centered theory of spatial reasoning. It is thus a source of encouragement to us to observe that it is knowledge of parties' policy reputations, not knowledge of politics in general, that is the key to whether (unlabeled) candidates get a reputational premium. But we have been candid. We did not start with the idea of a reputational premium when we designed our study. Replication is called for.

Replication is typically understood to mean repetition of identical procedures on an independent sample.[22] Much can be said for this conception of replication. All the same, we have adopted an

[22] See the special issue of PS: Political Science and Politics 1995, which is devoted to the issue of replication.

approach that, although similar in one respect, is quite different in another. Like the conventional approach, the test of the original finding is conducted on an independent sample. Unlike the conventional approach, the second test is different, in measures always, in design sometimes, from the first test.

This may seem a second-class strategy. If we fail to reproduce the original result, one plausible reason is simply that we used a different procedure the second time than we did the first. True enough, but our approach seems to us first-class rather than second just because it is riskier. If one really has got hold of something, and if one's understanding of what one has got hold of is on target, one should be able to carry out a different experimental procedure, yet observe an outcome that parallels the outcome observed in the first experiment. That is the rationale for Party Prototype Experiment.[23]

If a person knows what a party stands for, he will know the positions that candidates of the party typically take. It follows that one way to test whether people indeed know the positions that candidates of the party should take is whether they recognize when a candidate of a party has taken positions that he should *not* take. Accordingly, in the Party Prototype Experiment, we test whether respondents recognize that a candidate has taken stands at odds with those of the party whose banner he is running under.

Gathering an independent sample, we randomly asked one half of the sample:

Let me tell you about a person who says that he is a Republican. He supports more government spending and favors more rights for homosexuals. Would you say that he is a real Republican? while asking the other half of the sample:

Let me tell you about a person who says that he is a Democrat. He opposes more government spending and does not favor more rights for homosexuals. Would you say that he is a real Democrat?

In this study, we have two indicators of knowledge of politics in general: knowing how large a majority is required to pass a bill

---

[23] The Party Prototype Experiment was carried out in Study 11.

TABLE 3.5: Knowledge of Prototypical Party Positions

Constant	0.19
	(0.16)
Party ID	0.12
	(0.03)
Knows Reputations	0.82
	(0.15)
General Knowledge	0.14
	(0.09)
N	1463
Pseudo R-Squared	0.05

Note: Dependent variable takes a 1 if the respondent correctly identified the prototypical position of the political party and a 0 otherwise.

through the U.S. Senate, and knowing who is the prime minister of the United Kingdom. In addition, we have our measure of knowledge of the political parties' policy reputations, that is, knowing that the Republican Party is more conservative than the Democratic Party. Accordingly, we estimated equation (3.5) using our standard cast of actors:

$$\Pr(\text{Knows Proto-Partisan}_i = 1) = \varphi(\alpha + \beta_1 \text{PID}_i + \beta_2 \text{Reputations}_i + \beta_3 \text{Knowledge}_i) \qquad (3.5)$$

Table 3.5 presents the estimated coefficients from equation (3.5). The dependent variable is scored 1 if the respondent correctly rejects the candidate as a "real Republican (or Democrat)" and zero if the respondent incorrectly accepts the candidate as a prototypical Republican (or Democrat). The crucial issue is which measure enables citizens to recognize the typical party candidate: knowledge of politics in general or knowledge of the parties in particular. Again, the answer is that knowledge of the parties' policy reputations is statistically significant, while knowledge of politics in general is not.

In short, both the replication experiment and the original experiment demonstrate that knowledge of the parties' policy reputation specifically, not knowledge of politics in general, is key.

Sharing as Well as Knowing the Outlook of One's Party

A reputational theory of party identification suggests two conditions for a reputational premium. The first is that partisans must know the parties' policy outlooks to reward the candidate of their party for representing their party's program. Surely, though, partisans must also share the outlook of their party for a premium to exist.

The concept of a party supporter "sharing" the outlook of his party is open to multiple interpretations. Does it mean being in synch with the median legislative representative of the party or the median supporter? Does it mean agreement—however defined, with either over an array of policies, and if so, which ones? Or are there "signature" policies that define a party's policy reputation? Arguments can be made in favor of, and against, each of these operational specifications. For our part, we have chosen the most transparent meaning of sharing the outlook of one's party—transparent in two senses, we would add. A party's policy reputation refers to the ideological outlook of the party as a whole; and it is measured by an indicator used by all, or nearly so, who study public opinion American politics. Operationally, then, we characterize Democrats who classify themselves as liberals and Republicans who classify themselves as conservatives as sharing the outlook of their parties (or "sorted"). We characterize Democrats who either do not classify themselves as liberal or identify themselves as conservative, and Republicans who either do not classify themselves as conservative or identify themselves as liberal, as not sharing the outlook of their party (or "not sorted").[24]

The prediction then is, partisans who share the outlook of their party as well as know it will favor the candidate of their party in proportion to the strength of their identification with their party. We therefore estimate, for those who know the policy reputations of the parties, the following probit equation:

$$\Pr(\text{Vote}_i = L) = \phi(\alpha + \beta_1 \text{PID}_i + \beta_2 L \text{ closer}_i + \beta_3 \text{Sorted}_i + \beta_4 \text{PID}_i {}^* \text{Sorted}_i) \tag{3.6}$$

[24] In our studies, ideological orientation is measured by the location that respondents assign themselves on a 7-point scale. Positions 1–3 are defined as liberal; 4 as moderate or middle of the road; and 5–7 as conservatives. Since the dominant usage of sharing is discontinuous—one is either sorted or not—we follow established practice.

TABLE 3.6: The Relevance of Ideological Sorting

Constant	−0.36
	(0.18)
Party Identification	−0.07
	(0.04)
Left Candidate Closer	1.51
	(0.1)
Sorted	0.42
	(0.22)
Party Identification X Sorted	−0.13
	(0.05)
N	899
Pseudo R-Squared	0.53

Note: Dependent variable takes 1 if voted for left candidate and 0 if voted for right candidate. Regression run on the subset of respondents who know the correct ordering of the parties.

with all the terms as they were with the addition of Sorted, scored 1 for sorted partisans and 0 for unsorted partisans.

The crux of the question is whether, for partisans who pass the first hurdle of knowing the parties' policy reputations, the impact of party identification on candidate choice is stronger among those who share their party's programmatic outlook than among those who do not. The results in table 3.6 show that it does. Even after controlling for spatial proximity and orientation on the policy issue, the interaction between party identification and being sorted is plainly significant.

Figure 3.6 provides a graphic interpretation of the results from equation (3.6), showing the influence of party identification to be conditional on whether partisans are sorted or not. Consider first the results for partisans who do not share the outlook of their party—the left panel in the figure. Assuming, for the sake of exposition, that the left candidate is closer to the voter, the probability of supporting the left candidate decreases from 86 percent for strong Democrats to 75 percent for strong Republicans.[25] It would, perhaps, be unfair to say that party identification

[25] If, on the other hand, we assume that the right candidate is closer to the voter, the probability of supporting the left candidate decreases from 37 percent for strong Democrats to 30 percent for strong Republicans.

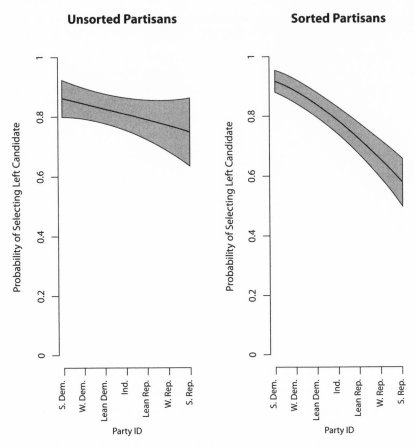

Figure 3.6: The Relevance of Ideological Sorting

is of absolutely no importance for partisans who do not share the outlook of their party—but it would not be excessively unfair.

The situation is quite different for partisans who do share the outlook of their party. There is a steep drop in support for the candidate on the left as one moves from strong Democrats to strong Republicans. Roughly, the probability of picking the candidate on the left differs by 35 points for strong Democrats and strong Republicans.

What do these results add up to? The candidates bear no party labels or markings. Yet programmatic partisans—that is, party supporters who know and share the outlook of their party—act as though the candidates' policy positions are proxies for their party affiliations. The result: parties' policy outlooks are part of their spatial calculations *even though there is no reference to parties.*

Finding that substantial numbers of party identifiers recover two pieces of policy information, one party-centered, the other candidate-centered, even though they are supplied with information only about the candidates' policy positions has deep implications for the neo-Downsian spatial model. If the finding is valid, the standard account is under-specified, focusing as it does solely on two instead of four pieces of information in the electoral choice. Accordingly, we conducted a replication experiment.

Replication: A Second Test of Pre-Coded Party Cues

The mechanism underlying our interpretation of the Downsian paradigm experiment is pre-coded party cues. The candidates do not have party labels. But the association between support for government spending and the Democratic Party and opposition to it and the Republican Party is stamped in the minds of programmatic partisans. Tell them the policy and they will know, from the reference to the policy alone, whether the candidate is likely a Democrat or a Republican. That is our hypothesis. Our objective is to administer a second, independent test of the hypothesis of pre-coded party cues. Just so far as policies are pre-coded, then a reference to an unbranded candidate backing a policy should convey the same information as a reference to a party-branded candidate backing that policy.

What might the expression "convey the same information" mean? The strictest definition is synonymy. Synonymy, spatially defined, cashes out in positioning candidates, based on the policies that they support, at the same point on a left-right policy dimension regardless of whether party labels are attached to them or not. Synonymy so defined indicates that a party brand or label to a candidate is superfluous information.

The irrelevance of party labels as informational sources is the intuition motivating the Superfluous Information Experiment. To carry out this experiment, we mounted a separate study ($N = 3,609$).[26] It is unreasonable to suppose that partisans have pre-coded any and every policy. But if the hypothesis of pre-coding is a useful one, it is fair to expect that they have pre-coded issues historically distinguishing the Republican and the Democratic parties.

So we focus on a pair of core issues—government spending and government assistance for the poor. The experiment features two manipulations. The first has to do with policy direction. Respondents are told of the positions of a candidate for Congress. One-half of the time, the candidate supports an increase in government spending and more government efforts to improve the social and economic position of the poor.[27] The other half of the time, the candidate opposes these policies. Half of respondents are thus randomly assigned to a candidate who takes liberal positions on two issues; the other half, to a candidate who takes conservative ones on the same two issues. The second randomized variation is the pivotal one. One-half of the time the candidate supporting liberal policies is identified as a Democrat and the candidate supporting conservative ones as a Republican. Then, in all experimental conditions, respondents are asked to place the candidate whose policies have been described (and sometimes whose party has been identified) on an 11-point scale of liberalism-conservatism.[28] In order to do this, they see on the screen a line anchored at one end by the label Extremely liberal and at the other Extremely conservative, with radio buttons to click at each of 11 equally spaced points.

We have christened this the Superfluous Information Experiment, since the centerpiece hypothesis is that, for programmatic partisans, attaching party labels to the candidates adds minimal spatial information above and beyond the description of their policies. The more similar the locations of candidates with and without party labels on the overall scale of liberalism-conservatism, the stronger the sense in which the labels provide superfluous information.

---

[26] Waves 7B, 7C, and 7D. See appendix B for Study details.

[27] Half the time, the specific reference was to Americans who are poor, the other half to African Americans who are poor. Making race explicit makes no difference.

[28] In the experiment, the scale runs from -5 (extremely liberal) to +5 (extremely conservative). In our discussion below, we re-scale so that the numbers run from 1 to 11.

TABLE 3.7: The Superfluous Information Experiment: Mean Placement of Candidates

| | Candidate Labels | | | |
	Liberal Candidate	Democratic Candidate	Conservative Candidate	Republican Candidate
Traditional Partisans	7.42 (0.17)	7.57 (.18)	4.51 (0.15)	4.39 (0.16)
Programmatic Partisans	2.25 (0.07)	2.28 (0.07)	9.48 (0.08)	9.55 (0.07)

Note: Standard errors in parentheses.

The columns in table 3.7 show the mean locations, for candidates with and without party labels, on a left–right scale running from 1 (most liberal) to 11 (most conservative). The rows show the scores of partisans who know the policy reputations of the parties and share the outlook of their party (bottom row), and those who satisfy neither criterion (top row).

Consistent with common sense, traditional partisans extract minimal information from the policies and the party labels. For example, they see a candidate who embraces two core liberal policies just to the left of center ($x = 7.42$). Pinning a party label on the candidate adds no information ($x = 7.57$). And the striking feature of these estimates—with or without party labels—is their variance (s.e. = .171 and .175, respectively). The same is true of their judgments of candidates backing core conservative policies. The mean location is just to the right of center with a party label (4.39) and without (4.51). Again, the size of the standard deviation is striking. In short, the policy signals convey scarcely any ideological information whether the candidates have party labels or not. Even after learning that a candidate supports a brace of core liberal (or conservative) policies, traditional partisans have no confident idea that they are liberal (or conservative).[29]

[29] Slightly more formally, differences in the mean placements of candidates with and without party labels are not statistically significant for traditional partisans.

Consider, in contrast, the judgments of partisans who know and share the outlook of their party. A Republican candidate who opposes government spending and government assistance for the poor they locate as definitely on the right—at 9.55, to be exact, and with a small standard error (.07). The key point, though, is they locate a candidate backing the same policies—but who does not actually bear the Republican label—at just the same point on the liberalism-conservatism dimension—at 9.48, to be exact, and with an indistinguishably small standard error (.08). And just the same is true on the other side of the political spectrum. Branded and unbranded candidates espousing liberal policies are located at 2.28 and 2.25, respectively, again with similarly small standard errors (.07 and .072, respectively).[30]

The lesson to draw from the Superfluous Information Experiment is thus an ironic one. Traditional partisans get no information from party brand names because they do not know what they mean. Programmatic partisans get no information from them because they already know what they mean.

Lessons from a Sterile Downsian Environment

For spatial theorists since Downs, two competitors take positions on a policy dimension. The competitors may be candidates. Or they may be parties. But it is never both candidates and parties. Our results show that partisans who know and share the outlook of their party recover information about the parties even when the only information that they are given is about the candidates.

This result fits the institutional logic of competition in American politics. One consequence of the separation of powers system is that competition takes place on two levels—candidate and party. And this result applies only to those who understand the ideological logic of the party system and are in sync.

[30] In all cases, these differences are statistically significant.

This result, however, raises an immediate question. What do they do with these four pieces of spatial information—the policy positions of the two candidates and the policy reputations of the two parties? Add them, divide them, take account of the distance between the candidates' positions with the programmatic orientation of his party—there are many possibilities. The objective of the next chapter, accordingly, is to specify the exact rule for combining these four pieces of information.

It is politics, not psychology, however, that concerns us. *In particular, we present a theory of how partisans take account of the parties' reputations as a function of the competing candidates' policy positions.*

CHAPTER 4

The Electoral Logic of Party Reputations

IN THIS CHAPTER, we present a theory of candidate positioning. The key to our account is the policy reputations of the two political parties. Candidates must take positions consistent with the policy reputations of their parties to collect a reputational premium. Our objective accordingly is to specify the rule or rules that define "consistent with."

Our job is twofold. The first task is to demonstrate that programmatic party identifiers favor candidates of their party on the grounds that they represent the overall outlook of their party, independent of the specific policy positions that the candidates take.[1] The second task is to specify the range of positions that a candidate may take and still be judged to represent the overall outlook of the party by supporters of his party who know and share its outlook. The two objectives are connected. The basis for the theory of candidate positioning that we shall advance is the new theory of party identification that we are proposing. Since it is a new theory of party identification, the burden of proof is on us. And the best way to demonstrate the heaviness of our burden, as it seems to us, is to make plain just how strong the evidence is in support of the canonical theory of party identification.

THE ERRORS-AND-BIAS INTERPRETATION OF PARTY IDENTIFICATION

On the established view, party identification represents an emotional attachment.[2] This attachment characteristically is acquired early in life, more or less unreflectively. Gilbert and Sullivan perhaps overstate just how early and just how unreflectively, when they quip:

[1] Provided, as we note below, that the candidates meet the Order condition.

[2] We say the canonical rather than classical view of party identification because the interpretation of *The American Voter* has regularly been reaffirmed, most notably, in Lewis-Beck et al. (2008) and Miller and Shanks (1996).

I often think it's comical—Fal, lal, la!
How Nature always does contrive—Fal, lal, la!
That every boy and every gal
That's born into the world alive
Is either a little Liberal
Or else a little Conservative?
Fal, lal, la![3]

Pre-adult socialization is the primary mechanism for acquisition of partisan loyalties. In other words, children and young adults learn to think of themselves as Democrats or Republicans through observation—and imitation—of their parents or peers. They do so painfully early—painfully, at any rate, for democratic theorists—often well before they have had an opportunity to develop their critical faculties or acquire a sense of politics and public affairs based on their own life experiences. Their parents—or in a stable party system, their parents' parents—may have had politically relevant reasons to identify with one party rather than another. But so far as they identify with the party of their parents or grandparents because it was the party of their parents or grandparents, their reasons are one, or two, or possibly more generations out-of-date. Copying is a method of learning. But it is a learning of political commitments without political content.

If party identification in its canonical conception lacks political content, just what does it consist in? "[A]n affective orientation to an important group-object in an [individual's] environment" is the admirably laconic answer of *The American Voter*:[4] Admirably laconic we say because all the work is being done by one word—"affective." Emotion, sentiment, feeling, the logic of party identification is the logic of the heart. True enough, the classical theory recognizes that voters may amend their party loyalties in moments of crisis. But even this concession is heavily qualified. The "updating" of party identification is done primarily by the cohort entering the electorate in response to dramatically new circumstances, not by those with already established loyalties. To a first approximation, to say party identification is to say party loyalty.

[3] Lolanthe, Act II. No. 14: Song "When all night long a chap remains." On the other hand, there is gathering evidence of a genetic basis of liberalism-conservatism. See, e.g., Alford, Funk, and Hibbing (2005) and Dawes and Fowler (2009).
[4] Campbell et al. (1960, 121).

And to say party loyalty is to say partisan bias. In the classic formulation of *The American Voter*:

> If party identification deeply influences the *partisan* character of a field of psychological forces, it also will have marked effects on the internal *consistency* of the field. Our conception of the role of partisan loyalties leads us to expect this result. Identification with a party raises a perceptual screen through which the individual tends to see what is favorable to his partisan orientation. The stronger the party bond, the more exaggerated the process of selection and perceptual distortion will be.[5]

Selective attention to information, and selective interpretation of the information attended to, are twin drivers of the "errors-and-bias" interpretation of party identification. This interpretation was put in memorably gracious terms by Donald Stokes. "[T]he tie between party identification and voting behavior," he remarked, "involves subtle processes of perceptual adjustment by which the individual assembles an image of current politics consistent with his partisan allegiance."[6] "Subtle processes of perceptual adjustment," less graciously put, cash out in errors and biases motivated by a desire to see their party in a favorable light and the opposing party in an unfavorable one.[7]

The partisan bias hypothesis has been incorporated into a more general model of motivated reasoning in politics. Integrating research on automaticity of responses and the primacy of affect in social psychology with experimental studies of political evaluation, Lodge and his colleagues,

[5] Campbell et al. (1960, 132–33).

[6] Stokes (1966, 127).

[7] There has been a friendly amendment to the traditional hypothesis of partisan reasoning, it is true. See Gerber and Green (1998); and Green, Palmquist, and Schickler (2002). The amendment is friendly in the sense that its proposers wish to retain the largest part of the conceptual furniture of the traditional interpretation of party identification, in particular, the linkage of partisan and social identities, and above all, the premise of the stability of party identification. But if the amendment is friendly in a number of respects, it turns the traditional interpretation of partisan reasoning on its head in another. For it involves a claim that partisan learning, so far from being biased, is rational—indeed, rational in arguably the strictest sense possible, namely, Bayesian updating. This claim of rational partisan learning, it will not be surprising to observe, has evoked in response a counter-claim that the very findings presented as evidence of rational learning are in fact evidence of biased reasoning (Bartels 2002). The statistical presumptions of Bayesian updating, a wag has observed, are themselves being updated. But this quip misses the genuine deepening understanding of rational updating that has followed from the renewed debate over partisan bias. See especially Bullock (2009).

among others, have presented strong evidence of a large family of biases in information processing. For example, the stronger an individual's attitude about a political issue, the more motivated they are to downgrade arguments at odds with his position on the issue, a disconfirmation bias, and to accept arguments in favor of it, a confirmation bias.[8] This tendency to believe that what one already believes is right, whatever one believes, is so strong that Lodge and his colleagues now speak of *The Rationalizing Voter*.[9]

The paradigm of motivated reasoning is far-reaching. It is not just a matter of liking those who like what we like and disliking those who dislike what we dislike. It extends to how we react to the facts of the matter. "Just the facts, ma'am" was the trademark expression of the classic police show, *Dragnet*. But in politics, though not just in politics, the facts of the matter do not always speak for themselves—even when there is a superabundance of information about them—because it is not just a matter of the facts but also of their interpretation.

In an ingeniously designed study, Brian Gaines and his colleagues (2007) investigated how partisans took on board information about two of the most thoroughly reported aspects of the Iraq war: troop casualties and the search for weapons of mass destruction (WMDs).[10] They carried out four studies, starting about six months after the invasion of Iraq and carrying on through transfer of power to the Iraqi provisional government, which show that both Democrats and Republicans "held reasonably accurate beliefs (about casualty levels and the failure to find WMDs) and seem to have updated them as circumstances changed."[11] But although Democrats and Republicans agreed on the facts of the matter, they were very far from agreeing on their meaning. Democrats typically characterized the casualty levels as very large or large, Republicans as moderate, small, or very small. And as for WMDs, when it became undeniable that they were not there, Democrats concluded that they never had been there, Republicans, that they had been moved or destroyed or not yet found.

---

[8] Taber and Lodge (2006).

[9] Lodge and Taber forthcoming.

[10] Gaines, Kuklinski, Quirk, Peyton, and Verkuilen (2007). See also Gaines, Kuklinski, and Quirk (2007).

[11] Gaines, Kuklinski, Quirk, Peyton, and Verkuilen (2007).

If the emotional forces bound up with party identification influence the meaning that partisans attach to the objective facts of the matter, they surely will shape perceptions of candidates and their positions. Who doubts that the more strongly that partisans identify with their party, the more likely they are to perceive a candidate of their party as representing their position on issues of the day? No doubt, various reasons might be given why partisans perceive the candidate of their party as holding positions akin to their own. The strength of their emotional attachment to the party may lead them to presume that the candidate of their party holds a position like their own. Or the process may work the other way around: again because of their identification of themselves with their party, they may presume that, because the candidate of their party holds a particular position, so do they. Either way, on the errors-and-bias interpretation of party identification, partisans are bad Downsians; and the stronger their partisanship, the worse Downsians they will be.

We propose to test the strongest version of the partisan bias hypothesis in spatial reasoning. Feeling an emotional attachment to a party, identifying one's self with it, predisposes party identifiers to perceive the candidate of their party as representing their position *even when there is unmistakable evidence before their own eyes that the candidate of the other party better represents their position.*

This hypothesis of partisan bias is the last thing from a straw man. It was in fact our own view, and not just at the outset of this project but also a good way through it.[12] For that matter, it was the view of anyone with whom we discussed the problem. Still, we felt that it would be an advance in knowledge—even if a modest one—to demonstrate via a randomized experiment partisan distortion in judgments of spatial proximity.

To test the hypothesis of radical misperception, we examine spatial judgments about two competing candidates. One is identified as the Democratic candidate, the other as the Republican candidate. The positions of the candidates are fully randomized, and identified visually with arrows drawn to a specific point on a 7-point scale. Thus, the experimental set-up is identical to the one from the last chapter, though here we brand the candidates with party labels. To test for partisan bias of spatial locations,

[12] More exactly, the view of one of us. See Van Houweling and Sniderman (2004).

TABLE 4.1: Partisan Bias in Spatial Judgments

Constant	0.5
	(0.06)
Party Identification	−0.31
	(0.01)
Democrat Closer	1.38
	(0.06)
N	3034
Pseudo R-Squared	0.4

Note: Dependent variable takes a 1 if the citizen prefers the Democratic candidate.

we estimate the following probit regression model of voter choice for respondents in the partisan condition:

$$\Pr(\text{Vote}_i = \text{Democrat}) = \phi(\alpha + \beta_1 \text{PID}_i + \beta_2 \text{Democrat closer}_i) \quad (4.1)$$

The results of the regression are reported in table 4.1. Both the partisanship of respondents and the identity of the nearest candidate are estimated to be highly significant determinants of choice. The negative coefficient for party identification indicates that Republican identifiers are less likely to select the Democratic candidate than Democratic identifiers. Similarly, the positive coefficient for the dichotomous proximity variable indicates that respondents are more likely to select the Democratic candidate when their self-location is closer to that of the Democrat.

Figure 4.1 displays a substantive interpretation of these estimates. The lines plot the probability that a person will choose the Democratic candidate conditional on which candidate is more proximate to the person and conditional on the person's partisan ties. They allow us to distinguish, for supporters of both parties, two types of choice situations. The first is when spatial and party cues are consistent; the second when they conflict.

Obviously enough, when the two cues are consistent, partisans will be overwhelmingly likely to declare that the candidate of their party represents their view on the issue. To take one example, our estimates indicate that strong Democrats will pick the Democratic candidate 94 percent of the time when the Democratic candidate is closer to them than the

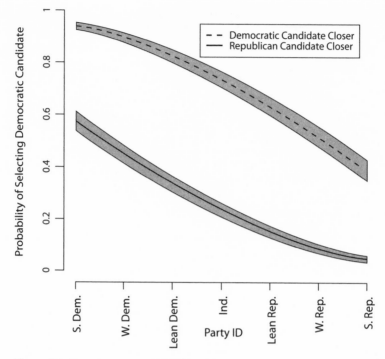

Figure 4.1: Partisan Bias in Spatial Judgments

Republican candidate.[13] Republicans mirror the behavior of Democrats. As figure 4.1 shows, strong Republicans will pick the Republican candidate approximately 95 percent of the time when the Republican candidate is closer to them. The vital question, though, is how do partisans behave when spatial and party cues conflict.

To judge from figure 4.1, party identifiers leap off the pages of *The American Voter*. An extraordinary proportion of them declare that the candidate of their party is closer to them *even when they are looking straight at incontrovertible evidence that the position of the candidate of the opposing party in fact is closer to their own position.* For example, strong Democrats will still pick their own party's candidate as representing their position 58 percent of the time, even when the position of the Republican candidate is closer to theirs. Strong Republicans are similarly

[13] Again, we want to underline that the numbers have no absolute meaning. They are relative to the test condition.

susceptible to errors in spatial judgment. A strong Republican will pick the Republican candidate as representing their position 62 percent of the time even when the position of the Democratic candidate is closer to the respondent than the Republican candidate. In short, our estimates indicate that respondent partisanship has a substantial impact on candidate choice.

"Substantial" understates the result, one could argue. The candidate's policy position is unambiguous and unequivocal. Yet, most who strongly identify with their party "misperceive" the candidate of their party as their spatial favorite when the position of the candidate of the other party, in fact, is closer to theirs. Here surely is evidence of partisan bias *in flagrante.*

THE CANONICAL THEORY OF PARTY IDENTIFICATION

Party identification is a matter of social identity that Angus Campbell and his colleagues (1960) originally proposed, a conceptualization that Green and his colleagues have subsequently extended.[14] Prototypical examples of social identities include "working" or "middle" class for Democrats and "people of means" and "business executives" for Republicans.[15] We

[14] See Green, Palmquist, and Schickler (2002) for a powerful statement of party identification as social identity. There is a subtle, but possibly consequential, difference, though, between their conceptualization and that of Campbell and colleagues. For the former, identification with a party, though a consequence of identification with a social group, is an autonomous and predominant force; for the latter, identification with a party is secondary to identification with a social group. For authoritative broad-gauge reviews, see Johnston (2006) and Jacoby (2010). For an excellent overview of the social identity approach in the context of comparative politics, see Bartle and Belluci (2009). We would also be remiss to not recommend Greene (1999, 2004), who offers an uncommonly clear account of the theoretical premises underpinning the treatment of party identification as a social identity.

[15] The social identity theory of party identification appeals to social identity theory in social psychology by way of securing a theoretical foundation. It is not altogether clear what work this appeal is doing. In the social psychological formulation, however, the signature feature of social identities is that they are situational and therefore fluid and transient. In the party identification literature, social identity is dispositional and enduring. For a sharp-edged analysis of the double barreled concept of social identity, see Huddy (2001, 2002). There also is a subtle, but possibly consequential, difference between the conceptualization of Campbell and colleagues and that of Green and colleagues. For the former, identification with a party, though a consequence of identification with a social group, is an autonomous and predominant force; for the latter, identification with a party is secondary to identification

agree that party identification is a matter of identity: but political rather than social identity. In American politics, the prototypical political identities are liberal Democrat and conservative Republican.

Conceptualization

Every theory of party identification of which we are aware presumes that partisans are cut from the same cloth. These theories differ only in their choice of material: "affective orientation" for one; "differential benefits" for another; "a running tally" for yet another; "social identity" for still another; and so on. Their disagreements have drawn all the attention; their point of agreement, none. And it is vital: theories of party identification have all agreed that whatever it means and however it works, it means the same thing and works the same way for all party identifiers.

A desire for generality is understandable, and often admirable. But when it comes to giving an account about reasoning and choice in politics, a one-size-fits-all theory has long seemed to us[16] a second-best strategy. There is more than one reason why it is a second-best strategy, but here is the first one that led us to this view.

> Imagine two hypothetical voters. One is exceedingly well informed about politics, a daily and devout reader of the *New York Times*, who follows closely the major issues of the day, both national and international. The second, a *Daily News* fan, is hardly overburdened by the amount of time, or effort, he devotes to public affairs—in fact, looks only at the sports page and cares next to nothing about politics. Is it plausible to suppose that these two voters, asked to make a choice about who should be president of the United States, would make up their minds in the same way?[17]

Just as it is unreasonable to presume that everyone goes about making up their mind the same way, so we contend that it is unreasonable to presume that being a Democrat or a Republican means the same thing for everyone. For some, identification with a party represents an "affective

---

with a social group. For an excellent overview of the social identity approach to party identification, see Bartle and Belluci (2009).

[16] "Us" refers to Sniderman.

[17] Sniderman, Glaser, and Griffin (1991).

orientation," a psychological attachment reinforced by emotion and habit. For others, their identification with their party includes identification with the outlook and policies that it stands for. For them, part of what it means to identify with one of the parties is to identify with a particular view of politics, and part of what it means to identify with a particular view of politics is to identify with a particular party.

Why speak of a "view of politics"—as opposed to particular policy preferences—and what does this notion of a view of politics entail? The partisan we have in mind aims to make the most of the choices on offer. He aims to realize his policy preferences all in all, or as many as are practical. The political parties organize the alternatives on offer. Thanks to their efforts, voters confront an organized menu of choices. In contemporary American politics, the menu as a whole is organized along ideological lines. One party offers a set of liberal policy alternatives; the other of conservative ones.

This all-in-all tendency of partisan alternatives to be organized on ideological lines is what we have in mind when we speak of a "view of politics." There are other possibilities, we recognize. The divergence between the parties on the traditional values agenda is one; their divergence on the social welfare agenda is another. We leave the advantages of these other views of a "view of politics" to investigate in the future, since there are no standardized measures of them at the present time. Here and now, by a view of politics, we mean a broadly liberal or conservative outlook on it.

From the classical view of party identification, it is heresy to speak of partisanship consisting of a conjunction or fusion of an ideological and an emotional attachment outlook on politics. The classical view of party identification argues for the similarity of party identification with religious attachments precisely on the grounds that both are acquired early in life, and more or less reflexively in response to parents and peers. As Warren Miller and Merrill Shanks write:

> In seeking to describe the nature of party identification without direct reference to politics, it is sometimes helpful to turn to the example of religion as a comparison that is much more than an analogy. Party affiliation, like religious affiliation, often originates within the family, where it is established as a matter of early socialization into the family norms. In addition to the primary group

experience, however, the maturing child has a clear sense of belonging to a larger body of adherents or co-religionists. The sense of self in the religious context is clearly established by the sense of "We are Roman Catholic," "I am a Jew"; in politics, "We are Democrats" or "I am a Republican."[18]

The aptness of the simile between partisan and religious identification has been taken for granted. In fact, however, it is instructive just by virtue of its inaptness. Children become Catholics and Jews by virtue of being raised as Catholics and Jews, indeed, characteristically, by receiving formal as well as informal schooling in the doctrines of their religion. Their understanding of the ideas, images, practices, values, and doctrine distinctively identified with their religion is limited, muzzy, and superficial as judged by the standards of priests or scholars, or informed opinion. All the same, to be a practicing Catholic is to have a certain view of the world and what lies beyond it. To be a practicing Jew is to have a different—not entirely but certainly distinguishable—view of the world and what lies beyond it.

Religious identification and belief are married. It is the divorce of party identification and belief that defines the canonical conception of partisanship. The partisan of *The American Voter* faithfully votes for his party's candidates, but has only a blowsy understanding of his party's fundamental political principles. Of course, the traditional partisan has political ideas. But characteristically they are loosely tied to one another, and still more loosely to identification with his party.

Ironically, the stock simile of party and religious identification is custom-tailored for the new theory of party identification that we are proposing. Just as the understanding of many adherents of the doctrines of their religion is imperfect, so too, the understanding of programmatic partisans of the principles of their parties is imperfect; even on points of consequence, they are sometimes wrong or out-of-step with opinions of the day. But they identify with the view of politics that their party is identified with. For a liberal Democrat, to be a Democrat is to be liberal and to be liberal is to be a Democrat. For a conservative Republican, to be a Republican is to be a conservative and to be a conservative is to be a Republican.

---

[18] Miller and Shanks (1996), 120.

Programmatic partisans know as well as share the outlook of their parties; traditional partisans neither know nor share the outlook of their parties; and, obviously enough, other party supporters fall somewhere between the two.

Operationalization

To operationalize our key concepts, we trade in the currency of the realm. Party identification and ideological self-identification have been measured time and again, mainly (though not always) in the same way from study to study.[19] The measures of partisanship and ideology therefore have sharply defined profiles. The same is true for our measure of knowledge of the political parties' ideological reputations. For all three indicators, what goes with what has been pinned down, literally over decades. So in each of our studies, we can tell whether (the largest number of) our measures measure what they purport to measure.[20] In short, plain vanilla indicators, one asking respondents to indicate whether they are a Democrat or a Republican, another whether they are liberal or conservative; yet another testing whether they know the parties' policy reputations.[21]

This trio is combined in three steps. First, party identifiers are classified as sorted (Republicans who also identify themselves as conservatives plus Democrats who also identify themselves as liberals) and nonsorted (all other partisans). Second, partisans are given a half point for being sorted and also a half point for knowing the policy reputations of the political parties. Summing their scores, the Index of Programmatic Partisanship runs from party identifiers who neither know nor share the outlook of their party, to those who manage one or the other but not both, to those who both know and share the outlook of their party. For presentational

---

[19] In fact, both have been assessed in branching and scalar (7-point) forms in previous research. Sometimes they are assessed in one format, sometimes in another, in our studies. Close comparison shows them to be interchangeable for our purposes. Results available on request. More generally, see Dennis and Li (2005). Consistent with recent practice, when presenting illustrative results we treat the NES party identification format as a two-category partisan variable (Democrat, Republican).

[20] See Cronbach and Meehl's (1955) classic—and neglected—analysis of validity.

[21] We use the standard NES measure of knowledge of party's policy reputations: "In general, thinking about the political parties in Washington, would you say that Democrats are more conservative than Republicans, or Republicans more conservative than Democrats?"

TABLE 4.2: Distributions of Traditional and Programmatic Partisans

	Type of Partisan		
	Traditional	Mixed	Programmatic
Knowledge Networks Study	15%	31	54
NES 2004	16	24	60
NES 2008	16	26	58

convenience, though, we shall refer to those who neither share nor know the outlook of their party as traditional partisans; those who manage one of these elements but not the other as mixed; and those who both know and share the outlook of their party as programmatic partisans.

Our focus throughout is on the difference in behavior between programmatic and traditional partisans. Mixed partisans, we suppose, exhibit behavior somewhere between traditional and programmatic partisans. Operationally, mixed partisans either know the outlook of their party but do not share it, or share it but do not know it. Linguistically, then, we sometimes speak as though there are three types of partisans—programmatic, mixed, and traditional. But here as elsewhere, our preference is to think in terms of differences of degree, not of kind.

How sizeable a portion of party supporters know and share the outlook of their party? Table 4.2 shows the proportions of traditional, mixed, and programmatic partisans. The first row reports the distributions from our first study, conducted in 2002; the second and third rows, the distributions from the NES 2004 and 2008.

The results from the three studies are similar, though not identical. In our central study, a little more than one-half of party identifiers qualify as programmatic partisans, while a little under one-fifth fall under the heading of traditional ones. In the 2004 and 2008 NES, the proportions of programmatic partisans are slightly larger—60 percent and 58 percent, respectively, while those of traditional partisans are almost the same size—16 percent. The similarities of the distributions across the surveys are reassuring. Our Knowledge Networks studies are not anomalies.

PROGRAMMATIC PARTISANS AND REPUTATIONAL PREMIUMS IN POLICY REASONING

To say that partisans are programmatic is to say that, in choosing between candidates running under the banners of the two parties, they will take account of the programmatic outlooks of the parties, quite apart from the actual issue positions of the two candidates.[22] We say "actual" because it is not our purpose to propose yet another errors and bias theory of party identification. For the purpose of hypothesis testing, accordingly, it is the actual positions of the candidates that count, not the ones that a partisan supporter might attribute to them by virtue of their identification with their party.[23] Hence our hypothesis: the more strongly that programmatic partisans identify with their party, the more likely they are to select the candidate of their party on the grounds that his policy position is consistent with the political outlook of their party. A natural test of this hypothesis is a predicted interaction between strength of party identification and fulfilling the conditions of being a programmatic partisan. Accordingly, we estimate:

$$\Pr(\text{Vote}_i = \text{Democrat}) = \phi(\alpha + \beta_1 \text{PID}_i + \beta_2 \text{Democrat closer}_i$$
$$+ \beta_3 \text{Programmatic index}_i + \beta_4 \text{PID}_i * \text{Programmatic index}_i) \quad (4.2)$$

where Democrat takes a 1 if the voter selects the Democratic candidate and a 0 otherwise; PID is the standard 7-point party self-identification variable; Democrat closer takes a 1 if the Democrat is the spatial favorite and a 0 otherwise; and Programmatic partisanship takes a 1 if the voter meets both of the conditions for programmatic partisanship, discussed above, a 0.5 if the voter meets one but not both of the conditions, and a 0 otherwise. To maintain some fidelity to political reality, we estimate this equation on the subset of respondents who face correctly ordered

[22] We leave open for future research the question of whether, in taking account of the programs of the parties, partisan attend to both or just one, and if one which one.

[23] Appendix A engages with this possibility in detail. In particular, the appendix shows that, even under ideal conditions, expressed citizen preferences respond weakly to candidate policy positions. It may be another matter, however, in the case of highly salient candidates who are highly attractive on other grounds.

TABLE 4.3: The Programmatic Conditions and Partisanship

Constant	0.81
	(0.2)
Party ID	−0.25
	(0.05)
Programmatic Index	1.24
	(0.11)
Democrat Closer	0.83
	(0.29)
Party ID X Programmatic Index	−0.34
	(0.07)
N	1257

Note: Results from probit regression. Dependent variable takes a 1 if the voter selects the Democrat and 0 otherwise.

candidates, with the Democratic candidate to the left of the Republican candidate.

The key difference between our theory and the canonical interpretation of party identification rests with the coefficient β_4. This coefficient captures the extent to which the influence of party identification is conditional on party identifiers knowing and sharing the outlooks of their party. This coefficient will take a negative sign, if our line of reasoning is right, with the negative sign indicating that party identification plays a more influential role in the choices of programmatic partisans.

The results, reported in table 4.3, strongly support our account. The influence of party identification is highly conditional on knowing and sharing the outlook of one's party. Indeed, judging by the magnitude of the coefficients, the results indicate that party identification has more than *twice* the influence for voters who meet the programmatic conditions compared to voters who do not. Party identification influences the decisions of voters who meet the reputation conditions far more heavily than it does the decisions of voters who do not. The difference between the two types of voters, it is worth underlining, holds *even after controlling for spatial preferences*. We control, that is, for whether the respondent prefers the Democratic or Republican candidate on spatial grounds. Programmatic partisans distinctively support the candidate of their party, even if he holds relatively distant views from them, in proportion to the strength of their identification with their party. And they do so, our results indicate, not by virtue of an emotional bond, but by virtue of an attachment to the programmatic outlook of their party.

CANDIDATE POSITIONING AND THE REPUTATIONAL PREMIUM: THE ORDER RULE

It is our claim that partisans who know and share the outlook of their parties take account of two types of policy information—the policy positions of the candidates and the policy reputations of the two parties under whose banner they are running. This claim fits with the results to this point. What we need to manage now—and need is the right choice of word—is to specify the combinatorial rule they follow in making use of both sources of policy information.

In a general way, it is obvious that the candidate of a party who takes a position that violates the policy reputation of his party risks the loss of the support of partisans who know and share the outlook of the party. But what does this mean, exactly? How far may a candidate deviate from the policy reputation of his party without losing the support of programmatic partisans? And, however broad or narrow the latitude that a candidate has in practice, what is the reason as a matter of theory that he can deviate so far, and no farther?

Several formulations are possible, depending on the ambitiousness of assumptions about citizen knowledge that one is willing to make. Our preference is for the least ambitious assumption. The rule defining when a candidate violates the policy reputation of his party that requires the least ambitious assumptions about citizen knowledge is this: As a candidate of the liberal party, the Democratic candidate must be more liberal than the candidate of the conservative party. As a candidate of the conservative party, the Republican must be more conservative than the candidate of the liberal party. More generally, party candidates must line up vis-à-vis one another in the same ideological order that their parties line up vis-à-vis one another—the "Order Rule," as we have dubbed it.

According to our theory, it is a necessary condition for a party candidate to comply with the Order Rule to collect a reputational premium. To say that it is a necessary condition is to say that any candidate who fails to satisfy it loses all benefit of the reputational premium. Our theoretical claim goes farther, though. Complying with the Order Rule is a sufficient as well as a necessary condition to collect a reputational premium. A candidate of a party need only line up vis-à-vis his opponent in the same ideological order as their parties line up vis-à-vis one another to collect a reputational premium. Our prediction is double-jointed, though. It not only specifies when candidates should receive a reputational premium, but also who should award it. If our reasoning is right, candidates who comply with the Order Rule trigger the party identification of programmatic partisans; candidates who fail to comply will receive no reputational premium from them. In contrast, traditional partisans, being insensitive to policy considerations, will not pay a reputational premium whether or not the candidates conform to the Order Rule.

To test this double-jointed hypothesis, we add two terms to our basic probit regression model of voter choice:

$$\Pr(\text{Vote}_i = \text{Democrat}) = \phi(\alpha + \beta_1\text{PID}_i + \beta_2\text{Democrat closer}_i + \beta_3\text{Order}_i + \beta_4\text{PID}_i{}^*\text{Order}_i) \qquad (4.3)$$

where Order takes on the value of 1 when the Republican candidate takes a policy position to the right of the Democratic candidate and 0 otherwise, and the interaction term (PID*Order) represents the impact of party identification conditional on the candidates being aligned in the correct ideological order.

The first column in table 4.4 focuses on traditional partisans. Clearly, party identification has a significant impact on their candidate preferences. The more strongly they identify with their party, the more likely they are to view the candidate of their party as representing their policy preferences. No surprise here. The question is whether traditional partisans take account of the order of candidate positioning. The canonical theory of party identification predicts that they do not. If they do not take account of the ideological order of the candidates, the interaction term between party identification and the Order Rule will not be significant.

And indeed it is not, as the first column of table 4.4 shows. To traditional partisans, it makes no difference if the Republican candidate is to the right of the Democratic candidate *or if the Republican candidate is*

TABLE 4.4: Activating Party Identification: The Order Rule

	Traditional Partisan	Mixed Partisan	Programmatic Partisan
Constant	1.07	−0.18	−0.18
	(0.21)	(0.14)	(0.11)
Party Identification	−0.49	−0.14	−0.12
	(0.07)	(0.04)	(0.02)
Democrat Closer	1.06	1.05	1.18
	(0.21)	(0.11)	(0.1)
Order	0.37	1.08	2.21
	(0.35)	(0.2)	(0.24)
Party Identification X Order	0.14	−0.19	−0.54
	(0.09)	(0.05)	(0.05)
N	337	727	1333
Pseudo R-Squared	0.45	0.34	0.48

Note: Results from probit regression. Dependent variable takes a 1 if the voter selects the Democrat and 0 otherwise.

to the left of the Democratic candidate. Traditional partisans are as likely to support the candidate of their party if he lines up on the wrong side ideologically of his opponent as on the right side. The main effect of party identification is strong and independent of the order of the candidates. Traditional partisans choose on the grounds of loyalty and emotional attachment to their party, not on the basis of whether the position of the candidate of their party is consistent with the political outlook of their party.

What about programmatic partisans? They know and share the outlook of their party. So they know and care whether the positions of the candidates are consistent with the policy commitment of the parties. Our prediction then is that the activation of party identification for programmatic partisans is conditional on the policy positions of the candidates conforming to the Order Rule. If the rule is satisfied, then the more strongly programmatic partisans identify with their party, the more likely they are to support the candidate of their party. But if the candidates do not conform to the Order Rule, the strength of identification of programmatic partisans is irrelevant.

The third column of table 4.4 makes plain that programmatic partisans award a reputational premium only if the candidates satisfy the Order Rule. Although the main effect of party identification is statistically significant, the magnitude of the coefficient is small—about four times smaller than the corresponding coefficient for traditional partisans. For programmatic partisans, almost the entire effect of party identification is conditional on candidates lining up vis-à-vis one another in the same ideological order as the parties line up vis-à-vis one another. Indeed, when the Order condition is met, judging by the coefficients, the importance of party identification increases fivefold for programmatic partisans.

The mixed partisans fall somewhere between the programmatic and traditional partisans. Although party identification exhibits some force when the candidates violate the Order Rule, it is a weak force, much less important than for traditional partisans. Similar to fully programmatic partisans, however, when the Order condition is met, the importance of party identification increases—though not nearly so dramatically as for the programmatic partisans.

ALTERNATIVE HYPOTHESES ON CANDIDATE POSITIONING

It is our claim that triggering party identification of programmatic partisans is conditional on party candidates conforming to the Order Rule. Our claim is not merely that candidates must obey the Order Rule to pocket a reputational premium. Our claim is that it is all they need to do to pocket it.

The first thing to say about our claim is that it is not self-evidently true. Consider the everyday use of ideological labels. "He is a conservative/liberal," we often say, meaning that he holds the principles of the political right/left. This categorical usage is a common, perhaps the most common, way that we use ideological labels. We can, and sometimes do, point to degrees of liberalism or conservatism. But pegging a position or candidate as liberal or conservative does the job we most often want done.

The categorical use of ideological terms points to an obvious objection to the Order Rule. Yes, party candidates must line up in the right order vis-à-vis one another—that is, in the same order as their parties line up—for their positions to be consistent with the political outlook of their party. But they must do more. A Democratic candidate must be liberal, not just more liberal than his Republican opponent. On this view, there is all the difference between a liberal Democrat facing off against a conservative Republican and a conservative Democrat doing the same against an even more conservative Republican. To win the support of Democrats who understand the ideological logic of the party system and share the ideological outlook of their party, Democratic candidates must locate themselves on the left—and not merely to the left—of their Republican opponents. Likewise for Republican candidates facing off against Democratic opponents.

An argument that candidates must line up on the appropriate sides, and not just in the appropriate order, is the last thing from a straw man. All the more reason, then, not to apply it mechanically to any and all party identifiers. Traditional partisans are bound by emotion and habit to their party, not the policy program of the party. This is not to say that they have no political ideas. It is to say that they do not organize their thinking around the ideological framework of the parties. Why, then, should their support for the candidate of their party be conditioned on whether he lines up on their party's side of the ideological divide or not? It is a quite different matter for programmatic partisans. They know the ideological logic of the party system. So they are in a better position to recognize when a candidate is on the wrong side of the ideological divide. And programmatic partisans share the ideological outlook of their party. So they have a reason to punish a candidate of their party who lines up on the wrong side of the ideological divide.

All of this has force, we recognize. But these directional claims rely on the abstractions of "left" and "right" sides. The abstractions come easily enough to one's lips. But their meaning is another matter. What does it mean to say that the Republican is on the "right" side of the policy space? Relative to what, one must ask? Relative to the "midpoint" of a left-right policy dimension, some might answer. Candidates located to the left of the midpoint are liberal; those to the right of it are conservative. But to commit to the position that there is an absolute midpoint is to make a deep commitment about the nature of a policy space. The midpoint is a fixed star, universally agreed on. But to move in this direction is to miss the deep contribution of theories of spatial reasoning. To judge relative distances—is San Francisco closer to Wichita, Kansas than it is to New York?—is easy. But to judge distances according to the Directional Theory—is Wichita to the west or east of the center of the country?—is hard. Our theory posits that voters compare the positions of party candidates *relative to each other*. If our theory is right, candidates who satisfy the Order Rule will collect a reputational premium, and they will do so whichever side of the ideological divide they position themselves on. Ultimately, we allow the data to judge whether our perspective has merit.

We test whether candidate order is a sufficient as well as necessary condition for a programmatic partisan to respond on a partisan basis by considering the following model:

$$\Pr(\text{Vote}_i = \text{Democrat}) = \phi(\alpha + \beta_1 \text{PID}_i + \beta_2 \text{Democrat closer}_i \\ + \beta_3 \text{Offside}_i + \beta_3 \text{PID}_i{}^*\text{Offside}) \qquad (4.4)$$

where Offside takes a 1 if the Democratic candidate positions himself to the right of center or if the Republican candidate positions himself to the left of center, and a 0 if both candidates take positions ideologically consistent with their parties' reputations. We maintain the central conditions for our theory—focusing on programmatic partisans, and only including choices in which the Democrat is to the left of the Republican.[24] Our objective is to upset our theory, to see whether the influence of party identification diminishes if a candidate moves "offsides." The Directional Theory posits that such a move matters a great deal; our theory posits that such a move, by itself, is inconsequential.

Are programmatic partisans more likely to respond as partisans when the candidate of the party of the left has lined up *on the left* and not merely to the left of the candidate of the party of the right? The answer, table 4.5 makes clear, is no. The interaction between party identification and offsides is not close to statistical or substantive significance. To programmatic partisans, it is unimportant whether a candidate is "offsides." So long as the candidates line up in the correct order, with the Democrat to the left of the Republican, programmatic partisans award the full reputational premium to the candidate of their party.

Still, it might be objected that races in which the candidates take the appropriate side can take many different forms. The candidate of the party of the left may be just barely to the left of the neutral point; alternatively, he may be crowding the left pole. The same holds for the candidate of the

---

[24] Notice that focusing on cases in which the Democrat is to the left of the Republican entails excluding cases in which *both* the Democrat and Republican adopt "offsides" policy positions.

TABLE 4.5: Activating Partisanship, Ordering, and Offsides

Constant	0.98
	(0.08)
Party Identification	−0.16
	(0.01)
Offside	−0.01
	(0.09)
Democrat Closer	0.23
	(0.02)
Party Identification x Offside	0.01
	(0.02)
N	703
Pseudo R-Squared	0.98

Note: Results from probit regression. Dependent variable takes a 1 if the voter selects the Democrat and 0 otherwise. The regression includes only programmatic partisans, and it only includes cases in which the Democrat is to the left of the Republican.

party of the right. Perhaps, then, it is not just a matter of whether candidates are on the opposing sides of the ideological divide. Perhaps it also is a matter of how far apart they are. The farther apart the candidates are, the easier it is to see that each represents the outlook of their party; the closer together they are, the harder it is to see this. If so, the more polarized candidates are, the better their chances of collecting a reputational premium.

The question then is, as the candidates move farther apart, are they more likely to collect a reputational premium? To ask about the effect of partisan polarization in the American party system is to ask about the effect of a candidate of the Republican Party moving toward the conservative pole and a candidate of the Democratic Party moving toward the liberal pole. There is no reason to expect that traditional partisans will take account of how polarized are the candidates' positions. After all, traditional partisans do not appear to care if the candidates reverse their order entirely; they appear almost blind to the candidates' policy positions. The critical test of the polarization conjecture, then, is whether, for programmatic partisans, the influence of party identification on candidate preference increases as the policy distance between the competing candidates increases. The answer is no, as the results in table 4.6 make plain.

TABLE 4.6: Polarization and Activating Partisanship

	Traditional Partisans	Programmatic Partisans
Constant	1.77	1.64
	(0.59)	(0.41)
Party Identification	−0.45	−0.63
	(0.14)	(0.09)
Democrat Closer	1.12	1.51
	(0.3)	(0.19)
Polarization	−0.13	0.11
	(0.2)	(0.15)
Party Identification X Polarization	0.03	−0.02
	(0.04)	(0.03)
N	169	703
Pseudo R-Squared	0.4	0.76

Note: Results from probit regression. Dependent variable takes a 1 if the voter selects the Democrat and 0 otherwise.

And the answer is no for programmatic partisans as well as traditional partisans. For both groups of partisans, the interaction between party identification and candidate polarization is not even close to significant.

Finding an absence of an interaction between party identification and candidate polarization speaks to a signature characteristic of the American party system, we believe. On all accounts of contemporary American politics, partisan legislators have moved to the ideological poles over the last thirty years. This agreed-on fact of ideological extremism at the elite level has raised a question. How can legislators take extreme positions when their supporters have remained moderate in theirs?

The results in table 4.6 suggest two observations. The first is that the traditional partisans are insensitive to the ideological positions of the candidate of their party because they are insensitive to the political outlook of their party. The second observation is that programmatic partisans are insensitive to the degree of polarization of the candidates for just the opposite reason: because they care about the ordering of the candidates and not their placement.

Even so, a reasonable person may respond, judgmental rules rarely are knife-edge. It must matter, he would say, whether the Order Rule is violated flagrantly or by just a smidgen. Perhaps the lack of significance in the polarization regression stems from some quirk of the variables. Perhaps it matters, for example, on one side of the rule but not the other—that is, perhaps partisanship increases with the distance between the candidates, but only so long as they line up in the correct order. Or perhaps just the opposite.

Consider therefore another test of the Order Rule. We first subtract the Republican position from the Democratic position. Since higher values correspond to more spending, any positive difference means that that Democrat is to the left of the Republican—that is, he wants more spending than the Republican candidate. This candidate difference score, thus, runs from −6 to 6, with −6 representing extreme polarization, but with the Republican to the left of the Democrat; positive 6, by contrast, represents conventional polarization, where the Democrat is far to the left of the Republican. We then estimate a now-familiar equation, interacting this candidate difference score with party identification, and controlling for Downsian proximity. The main difference in this equation is that we include the difference score as a series of dummy variables rather than as a continuous variable. This allows us to examine each value of the score carefully, and to see whether a sharp break in partisan behavior occurs when the candidates cross over each other. We focus on programmatic partisans.

We use a figure to report the results.[25] In figure 4.2, we plot the predicted probability of selecting the Democratic candidate as a function of the difference in positions between the candidates for programmatic partisans.[26] The grey lines around each predicted probability represent 95 percent confidence intervals. Recall that, for all distance scores less than 0, the Democrat is to the right of the Republican and the Order Rule is violated; for all values greater than 0, the Order Rule is satisfied.

The key result from this figure is this: for all negative values of candidate distance, Democrats and Republicans behave almost identically—and they do not vary their behavior as the distance increases. Though the point estimates bounce around, members of both parties select the Democrat about 65 percent of the time regardless of the distance between

[25] The presence of many dummy variables results in an unwieldy table. Contact the authors for a copy of the table.

[26] We arbitrarily assume that the Democratic candidate is closer to the respondents for the simulations used to produce the predicted probabilities. This explains the modest bias in favor of selecting the Democratic candidate in the figures.

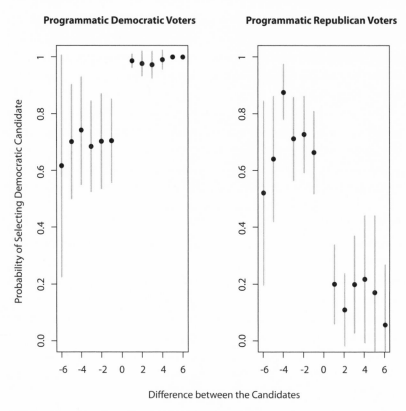

Figure 4.2: The Order Rule—A Knife-Edge Result

the candidates: partisanship does not matter when the Order Rule is vio-lated. Instead, citizens revert to the Downsian state of nature, basing their choice largely on which candidate is closer. Moreover, the probability of selecting the Democrat does not depend on whether the distance score is −6 or −1—in all cases, about 65 percent of partisans, both Democrats and Republicans, support the Democratic candidate.

By contrast, as soon as the candidate distance score becomes positive—indicating that the Democrat is to the left of the Republican—partisanship kicks in sharply. Democrats support the Democratic candidate with nearly probability 1; Republicans support the Republican candidate roughly 85 percent of the time.[27] We thus observe a marked jump in partisanship as

[27] Recall that this asymmetry is a result of assuming that the Democratic candidate is closer to the citizen in the simulation.

soon as the candidates order correctly. At the same time, however, this manifestation of partisanship does not increase as the distance between the candidates increases. It is a knife-edge result that occurs just when the Order Rule is satisfied.

Before we move on, we note that the Order Rule is not as counterintuitive as it may initially appear. The intuition is, in fact, not so far from the intuition that drives standard Downsian reasoning. Notice that if the candidates satisfy the Order Rule, the Democratic candidate is located closer to the core Democratic platform and the Republican candidate is located closer to the core Republican platform.[28] If voters were asked, that is, which candidate, the Democrat or the Republican, is more likely to support the core Democratic agenda, they would intelligently respond "the Democrat" when the Order Rule is met. When the Order Rule is violated, however, this simple equation no longer holds, for now the Republican candidate is actually relatively aligned with the core Democratic agenda.

The Order Rule thus operates as follows. If a candidate of a party takes a position consistent with—in the specific sense that we have defined consistent— the programmatic outlook of his party, he will receive support premium from supporters of the party who know and share its outlook in proportion to the strength of their identification with it. If the candidate violates the Order Rule, he receives no reputational premium, however minor his violation of the rule.

REPLICATION: THE ORDER RULE

If candidates line up in the right order, they get a reputational premium. What is more, they pocket the premium whatever side of the ideological continuum they line up on, and however far to one side they locate themselves, provided the candidates line up in the appropriate order. This follows from our claim that programmatic partisans evaluate whether candidates stand with their party not by comparing their positions with an abstract standard, but by comparing their positions vis-à-vis one another with the positions of the parties vis-à-vis one another.

[28] This, at least, is true in the modern political environment, in which the parties adopt highly polarized platforms.

This Order Rule has the virtue of simplicity—not a small virtue considering how modest is the knowledge of politics even of relatively knowledgeable citizens. The rule also has the virtue of ecological validity. Voters must choose between the alternatives on offer at each election. In a party system polarized at the level of party leaders and sorted at the level of party supporters, the Order Rule produces the best informed choice for partisans who share the outlook of their party.

Still and all, obtaining a finding that fits the theory using the data set that one used to develop the theory is not dispositive. Replication is required. The replication standard that we have set is reproducibility, in an independent data set, using different procedures that should yield a similar result if the underlying reasoning is right.

In both the original and the replication studies, the candidates bear party labels and are assigned randomly to all possible positions (except for ties). That is the fundamental point of similarity. But there are two points of dissimilarity in measurement. In the first study, the issue was the appropriate level of government services and spending. In the replication study, it is government regulations on business to protect the environment.[29] In the first study, the dependent variable was, which candidate's position on the issue represents the position of the respondent on the issue. In the replication study, it is which candidate's position on the issue represents the respondent's "general outlook on politics."

On the basis of the findings of our first study, we expect three results in the replication study. First, partisanship and candidate preference are more closely tied together for programmatic partisans than for traditional party identifiers when the candidates have lined up in the appropriate order, and the other way around when they have not. Second, it should be irrelevant for traditional and programmatic partisans, albeit for different reasons, whether the candidates line up on the appropriate sides, as distinguished from the appropriate order. Third, it should also be irrelevant how far to one or the other side they line up, provided again that they line up in the appropriate order.

Table 4.7 shows the correlation between party identification and candidate preference, conditional on whether the candidates are lined up in the appropriate order or not, and in both cases, the absolute distance

---

[29] The replication experiment was conducted in Study 11.

TABLE 4.7: Correlations between Party Identification and Candidate Preference

		Absolute Distance Between the Candidates					
	Order Rule	1	2	3	4	5	6
Traditional Partisans	Violated	−0.45 (45)	−0.47 (39)	−0.25 (41)	−0.06 (23)	−0.61 (12)	−0.87 (3)
	Satisfied	−0.51 (58)	−0.46 (47)	−0.4 (37)	−0.58 (23)	−0.5 (22)	— (11)
Mixed Partisans	Violated	−0.38 (123)	−0.36 (114)	−0.09 (88)	−0.14 (40)	−0.05 (27)	−0.63 (13)
	Satisfied	−0.5 (102)	−0.55 (97)	−0.68 (86)	−0.65 (55)	−0.3 (26)	−0.4 (17)
Programmatic Partisans	Violated	−0.15 (180)	−0.04 (156)	−0.11 (117)	0.03 (83)	0.09 (63)	0.17 (31)
	Satisfied	−0.73 (191)	−0.83 (170)	−0.8 (143)	−0.87 (104)	−0.86 (89)	−0.75 (27)

Note: Number of observations in the cell noted in parentheses.

between their policy positions.[30] The correlations are presented separately for traditional partisans, mixed and programmatic partisans.

Three findings stand out. For all practical purposes, it is irrelevant to traditional partisans whether the candidate of their party is in the appropriate order, or is on the appropriate side, or takes a position on the appropriate side closer to the pole or nearer the middle. Programmatic partisans care entirely about whether the candidate of their party conforms to the Order Rule. If he does, their partisan reaction is as strong as it could possibly be. On the other hand, if the candidates do not line up in the right order, there is no partisan reaction on their part. Mixed partisans—that is, party identifiers who either know the outlook of their party or share it but not both—fall in-between traditional and programmatic supporters. On the one hand, their partisan reaction is strongest when the candidates conform to the Order Rule, though not as strong as the reaction of programmatic partisans. On the other, there is some willingness on their part to tolerate marginal violations of the Order Rule.

[30] Only respondents identifying themselves as Democrats or Republicans were included in Study 11. The party identification measure thus can take on one of four values: strong Democrat, weak Democrat, weak Republican, strong Republican. We are presenting the data in this form in order that the results are transparent.

When Candidate Positions and Party Reputations Conflict

In a party system in which party leaders are polarized and party support-ers sorted, choices of candidates on the basis of their position or on the basis of their party's policy reputation characteristically coincide. But not always. Every now and then, the Republican candidate will be the spatial favorite of liberal Democrats; the Democratic candidate, the spatial fa-vorite of conservative Republicans.

In contests where candidate-centered and party-centered policy cues point in opposite directions, how will party supporters choose? Will party identification count for more in the choices of traditional or of program-matic partisans? On our theory, programmatic partisans place their bets primarily on policy outcomes on the basis of the programs of the parties rather than the positions of individual candidates. It is not necessary for them to have a theory of party government to adopt this reasoning, and quite possibly most do not. All that is necessary is to treat the political outlook of the party as a better predictor of policy outcomes than the po-sitions of individual candidates and to be concerned about realizing their preferences all in all rather than piecemeal, issue by issue.

If this line of reasoning is right, programmatic partisans should rely more heavily on party identification. That is, to realize their policy pref-erences all in all given the institutional reality of American politics, they should weight the party-centered cue over the candidate-centered one. To test our reasoning, we examine candidate preferences when the can-didates are lined up in the appropriate order and the candidate of the opposing party is the voter's spatial favorite. We estimate the following equation:

$$\Pr(\text{Vote}_i = \text{Democrat}) = \phi(\alpha + \beta_1 \text{PID}_i + \beta_2 \text{Programmatic index}_i + \beta_3 \text{PID}_i * \text{Programmatic index}_i) \quad (4.5)$$

where Democrat takes a 1 if the voter selects the Democratic candidate and a 0 otherwise; PID is the standard 7-point party self-identification variable; and the programmatic index takes a 1 if the voter both knows and shares the outlook of his party, 0.5 if the voter meets only one of these

TABLE 4.8: Conflicting Candidate and Party Cues

Constant	0.91
	(0.18)
Party Identification	−0.16
	(0.04)
Programmatic Index	0.64
	(0.36)
Party Identification X	−0.21
Programmatic Index	(0.07)
N	320
Pseudo R-Squared	0.25

Note: Results from probit regression. Dependent variable takes a 1 if the voter selects the Democrat and 0 otherwise. Run on the subset of observations for which the candidate from the opposing party is the Downsian favorite and the candidates line up in the correct order.

conditions, and a 0 otherwise. We focus on the sample for which the order condition is satisfied and for which the candidate from the opposing party is closer to the citizen—we focus, that is, on cases in which the party cue conflicts with the candidate placement cue.

The key result in table 4.8 is the test of an interaction between being a programmatic partisan and the influence of strength of party identification. If the interaction is significant, it is strong evidence in support of our hypothesis, since it indicates that party identification has a stronger influence over the choices of programmatic partisans than over those of traditional ones. The interaction is indeed statistically significant. When spatial and party cues conflict, programmatic partisans give more weight to the party affiliation of the candidate than do traditional partisans. Judging by the coefficients, programmatic partisans place about twice the weight on party identification in this circumstance than traditional partisans.

CAVEAT LECTOR

Programmatic partisans, we claim, support the candidate of their party above and beyond the congruence of their position with hers. They pay a premium in support in proportion to the strength of their identification with their party. But their awarding of a premium is conditional on the candidate of their party taking policy stands consistent with the reputation of their party—hence our characterization of it as a reputational premium.

Much hinges on specifying the meaning of the relation, "consistent with." Of the various possibilities, we have proposed the Order Rule. Candidates take positions consistent with the reputations of their party if, but only if, the candidate of the party of the left is to the left of the candidate of the party of the right. This is both a necessary and sufficient rule for candidates to follow in order to pocket a reputational premium, we have claimed. All our results, both those that we have presented and those that we have not, are consistent with this claim. And the simplicity and ecological validity of the Order Rule provide a theoretical base for our claim. It is an extreme claim all the same. Future research or further analysis may call for modification. Consequently, it is our bet that, if modification is necessary, it will be minor.

Whether we win or lose our bet, the findings of the last two chapters drive home the need to change standard practice. In the analysis of voting and policy preference, it is customary to ask whether ideological identification makes an explanatory contribution above and beyond that of party identification. Accordingly, the standard multivariate analysis treats the two as independent predictors. This presumes, however, that ideological outlook and party identification are separate and unrelated. In fact, they are locked together for the largest number. A majority of Democrats, and a still larger majority of Republicans, know and share the outlook of their party. For them, to be a Democrat (or Republican) means to believe certain things, and the other way around. To fail to recognize the conjunction or fusion of ideology and party is to miss the temper of contemporary American politics.[31]

---

[31] Habits die slowly, though. For a research program that aims to provide a theory of ideology as separate and unrelated to party, see Kinder and Kalmoe (2010). From our perspective, to examine ideology independent of party idetification approximates making steak Bercy without white wine and shallots.

CHAPTER 5

The Democratic Experiment

A SUPPLY-SIDE THEORY OF POLITICAL IDEAS
AND INSTITUTIONS

PINNING HIS RHETORICAL FLAG to his scholarly mast, V. O. Key Jr. (once) famously wrote: "The perverse and unorthodox argument of this little book is that voters are not fools."[1] Perverse was exactly the right choice of words. In the study of public opinion, the smart money has always bet against the political competence of ordinary citizens.

A quote from the sage of public opinion, Walter Lippmann, frequently kicks discussion off on a high literary note, something like:

> The individual man does not have opinions on all public affairs. He does not know how to direct public affairs. He does not know what is happening, why it is happening, what ought to happen.[2]

Certainly, there is no lack of quotable quotes to the same or similar effect; nor any lack of empirical studies, for that matter, documenting the ordinary citizen's minimal knowledge of, and interest in, public affairs. Then again, the one thing worse than having an argument that is too weak is having one that is too strong. Listen again to the wisdom of Walter Lippmann:

> [A]lthough public business is my main interest and I give most of my time to watching it, I cannot find time to do what is expected of me in the theory of democracy; that is, to know what is going on and to have an opinion worth expressing on every question which confronts a self-governing community. *And I have not happened to meet anybody, from a President of the United States*

[1] Key (1966).
[2] Lippmann (1927).

to a professor of political science, who came anywhere near to embodying the accepted ideal of the sovereign and omnicompetent citizen.[3]

It is arguable that it is a more wrenching admission for Walter Lippmann to acknowledge that he himself falls short of the knowledge required of a democratic citizen than that a president of the United States does. What is not arguable is that something has gone terribly wrong with the way that the question of political competence itself is being formulated if neither one of them can manage even a Gentleman's C.

How to think more productively about the democratic experiment and political competence is the subject of this chapter. As a first step, we will conduct a brief parade of our theory and findings, partly for the purpose of summing up, but mainly with an eye to clearing the ground for a broader discussion. Then, we mean to bring out the implications of both the theory and the findings for a supply-side theory of political competence. For our finale, we present a nice irony of democratic politics. It is well-known that limited knowledge of voters frees up elected representatives to act as they wish with minimal fear of electoral punishment. It is less well-known, though no less important, that understanding as well as ignorance of the big picture of American politics allows elected representatives a freer hand in playing the policy cards they wish to play and still win the backing of supporters of their party.

A Reputational Theory of Party Identification and Policy Reasoning

The identification of classical partisans with their party is tied to the fact that it was the party that their parents or peers identified with. It does not follow that they are merely emotional or psychological robots, however. Their heads are not empty of political ideas. They are concerned about their country and its future. They are not blind to outstanding candidates from the opposing party. Nevertheless, in the main and over the long haul, these classical partisans stand loyally by their party, casting their vote on the basis of habit and emotional attachment, not considerations of policy, still less an overarching or broad outlook on politics.

[3] Lippmann (1927); italics ours.

These partisans who appear on the pages of *The American Voter* and its successor, *The New American Voter*, remain a political force. Yet, as an overwhelming body of research now testifies, a signature fact of contemporary American electoral politics is the conjunction or fusion of party identification and policy preferences. Hence the need for a theory of party identification that incorporates policy preferences.

It is the strength of the rational choice approach to recognize the importance of policy preferences. Yet, in the contemporary neo-Downsian analysis of American elections, it is policy preferences on a miniature scale: notably, the policy preferences of candidates. Candidates' policy preferences remain an important component of the competition for electoral support. And to repeat again, it is the conjunction or fusion of party identification and policy preferences that is a signature feature of contemporary American politics. Hence the need for a party as well as candidate-centered theory of spatial reasoning.

A foundational premise of our reputational theory of party identification and spatial reasoning is that large numbers of party identifiers take account of the programmatic commitments of the parties in choosing between candidates on the basis of policy. This premise, if valid, entails taking account not just of two pieces of information, as the neo-Downsian account contends—namely, the policy positions of the candidates—but an addition of two more pieces of information—namely the policy reputations of the parties under whose banners the candidates are running.

Four pieces of policy information, not two, are taken into account. Indeed, to put our claim more strongly, if the policy positions of the candidates are consistent with the programmatic outlook of their parties, two pieces of information—the policy positions of the candidates—serve as signals of the two other pieces of information—the policy reputations of the parties—and vice versa.

This is what the "sterilized" Downsian experiment in chapter 2 demonstrated. Respondents, you will recall, see the policy positions of two competing candidates. The candidates' positions are crystal-clear. They are immediately comprehensible. And that is the sum total of the information that voters have to work with. They deliberately are not told the names of the candidates, since names can be indirect cues to their party affiliation; nor anything of their personal biography, for the same reason; nor anything of their political experience, again for just the same reason. Instead, the candidates are simply denominated candidate A and candidate B, and voters are asked to choose one who best represents their position on the issue. The design of the Downsian experiment thus accomplishes two goals in one stroke. Voters have *all* the information that candidate-centered theories of policy-voting posit that they use. And they have *only* the information that these theories stipulate that they use. No distractions; no misinformation; no uncertainty; no complexity—the contemporary neo-Downsian theory could not ask for more ideal conditions.

And yet, to borrow an adage of a revered colleague, "That's just theory; it doesn't have to be true."[4] As it happens, the candidate-centered theory is true. Voters do take account of the policy positions of the candidates in choosing between them. But, as the Sterilized Downsian experiment demonstrated, significant numbers of them do two additional things: (1) voters infer the party affiliations of the candidates from the policy positions that they take; and (2) when choosing the candidate who represents their position on a policy issue, many make use of all four pieces of information: the policy positions of the candidates they saw and the party affiliations of the candidates that they inferred from the candidates' policy positions.

The all-important question, however, is: What difference does it make that policy-guided choices between candidates are party-centered as well as candidate-centered? The answer is that candidates can get a bonus in support above and beyond the support they get from taking particular policy positions. They get this bonus in return for taking policy positions consistent with the policy reputation of their party—hence the term "reputational premium." Specifically, party supporters award a candidate of their party for taking positions consistent with the reputation of their party in proportion to the strength of their identification with their party. The more strongly they identify with it, the bigger the premium.

The concept of a reputational premium driven by strength of party identification is a study in irony, we acknowledge. Party identification is classically conceived as an emotional attachment, a matter of feeling and self-concept and sentiment. What is more, party identification is viewed as a primary source of a spider web of errors and biases in political per-

---

[4]The colleague is Raymond Wolfinger.

ception and inference. For many analysts, to say party identification is to say partisan bias. To contend that party loyalty has a multiplier effect increasing the impact of policy preferences on voting risks gives the impression of an oxymoron—or still worse, of being deliberately perverse and contrary and, in a phrase that should be retired from use, disproving the conventional wisdom.

But this impression of perversity is wrong all the way down. Our study has produced finding after finding in support of both the classical conception of party identification and the canonical candidate-centered theory of spatial reasoning. However, discovery of a reputational premium brings out from the shadows the role of party identification—under specifically defined conditions—in increasing the importance of the programmatic outlook of the parties in choices between candidates. And what are those conditions? That party supporters know and share the programmatic outlook of their party and that candidates of their party take positions consistent with the party's programmatic outlook.

The reasoning underpinning the condition that party supporters know and share the outlook of their party is straightforward. The reasoning pinning down the precise meaning of candidates taking positions "consistent with" the programmatic outlook of their party is not straightforward at all. Modeling a calculus of choice involving only two pieces of information—the policy positions of two competing candidates—has proven an increasingly complex business as analysis has progressively taken into account an increasing number of considerations—ambiguity in candidates' positions, for one; the consistency of their positions in the current election with those of previous elections (e.g., "flip-flopping") for another; and the role of political institutions (e.g., divided government) in shaping the policy outcomes of elections taken as a whole, for still another. Against this background of ever-increasing complexity, it would be too much to expect that a discovery that many voters are making use of not two but four pieces of policy information will be welcomed with huzzahs on all sides.

It follows that a primary responsibility of the account that we are proposing is to specify a spatial algorithm that defines how the policy positions of the candidates are combined with the policy reputations of their parties. On theoretical grounds, we have chosen a party-centered version of the Downsian proximity rule. To receive a reputational premium, a candidate's position on a policy must be closer to the overall outlook of his party than the position of the candidate of the opposing party. More formally, candidates must line up vis-à-vis one another in the same ideological order as their parties line up vis-à-vis one another.

The Order Rule is obviously a necessary condition of taking a position "consistent with" the policy reputation of one's party. The candidate of the party of the left must be to the left of the candidate of the party of the right. It is our claim, however, that the Order Rule is also a sufficient condition of taking a position "consistent with" the policy reputation of one's party. There are credible alternatives. All that we would emphasize here is that we have ruled them out not on theoretical but on empirical grounds. Knife-edged rules are not the rule in the real world of politics, where information is less readily available and more equivocal than in our contrived experiments.

These, then, are the key components of the reputational theory of party identification and spatial reasoning that we are proposing: the concept of a reputational premium and the Order Rule—that is, the spatial algorithm defining when the positions of a candidate are consistent with the programmatic outlook of his party.

A Party-Centered Supply-Side Approach to the Question of Citizen Competence

An ideology offers an expansive account of politics. It defines consistency in politics, picking out what goes with what. It supplies a master narrative that illumunates logical—or seemingly logical—linkages of combinations of preferences across policy domains. So defined, ideologies seem out of the reach of the ordinary voter. A half century of public opinion research has demonstrated that the ordinary citizen has minimal knowledge of politics and a minimal measure of the political sophistication necessary to connect the ideas, premises, and values that make up a wide-ranging belief system.

Downs famously provided a defense of rational ignorance, it is true. Even though voters know little, he argued that they know enough to choose rationally, and so, he went on to argue, it is rational for them to remain largely ignorant of politics, as indeed they are. This is not an obviously compelling argument on Downs' own principles. The sticking point is illustrated by the infamous turnout paradox. The probability of an individual voter deciding an electoral outcome is so low that the benefits gained by voting cannot outweigh the costs of turning out to vote, however modest the costs may be. But if there is no strictly rational basis to pay the costs of turning out to vote, there is no strictly rational basis for voters to pay the costs of acquiring even the minimal information necessary to make rational voting choices—that is, the policy positions of the candidates, however modest the cost of acquiring information about their policy positions.

Our aim has been to test the value of a party-centered theory of spatial reasoning. Taking a supply-side approach puts problems of information acquisition in a different perspective. Political parties are information broadcasters—or more accurately perhaps, information advertisers. They are in the billboard business, we have said, and, we would add, every other advertising business as well.

Advertising is an instructive metaphor. For one thing, it brings out the artificiality in politics of the distinction between belief and emotion. Each feeds off the other. A successful advertiser gets people to think what he wants them to think by getting them to feel what will encourage them to think it. And he gets them to feel what he wants them to feel by encouraging them to think what will lead them to feel what he wants them to feel. Belief excites emotion. Emotion reinforces belief. For another thing, successful advertising gets you to retain information that you have little intrinsic motivation to remember. Who, provided they are of an appropriate age, fails to automatically associate Cadillac cars and luxury. So, too, is it with political parties, with the difference that, here, advertising works to impart knowledge of a party's attributes.

Perhaps most fundamentally, though, the metaphor of advertising brings out the strategic utility of information. Political parties need to bind current supporters to their cause. And they need to add new supporters. How can they accomplish both? By advertising their wares. In contemporary politics, ideological outlooks have become part of the very identities of the parties, each appealing to its outlook when it is to its advantage and focusing attention on the outlook of the other party when it is to the disadvantage of the other party.

Why a party-centered focus? Citizens now enjoy easy access to a huge menu of informational (and entertainment) alternatives. Political parties have comparative advantages in this competition for attention for voters who identify with them because they provide the mechanism par excellence interlocking supply and demand. On the supply side, parties have strong incentives to be information broadcasters and stand out as a focal point of attention for voters who identify with them. On the demand side, party identifiers who are emotionally attached to their party and know and share its outlook have the motivation to pay the costs of acquiring party-relevant information on a continuing basis.

Political parties make two additional contributions on the supply side that deserve to be written in red ink. The first is that they help organize the choice space: they delimit, bundle, and brand the number of alternatives on offer. Our point is not that parties optimize electoral choice—by some criteria they may, by others not—but rather that they make it manageable.

At the most fundamental level, manageability of choices cashes out in co-ordination of alternatives—at the limit, to use the term of art, unidimensionality of policy choices. Rational choice studies of spatial reasoning have proceeded on the assumption of candidates competing on a unidimensional left-right continuum. This presumption of a single policy dimension has been an assumption of convenience. Calculation of a dominant policy position in a multidimensional space has not been tractable.[5] At the level of legislative voting, however, a mountain of analyses has established the unidimensionality of voting choices and the alignment of this comprehensive left-right dimension with partisanship.[6]

The role of the political parties in minimizing the dimensionality of choice spaces in legislatures remains an issue of intense interest—and debate. Of equal interest, and virtually no debate, is the role of political parties as the organizational instrument for minimizing the dimensional-

[5] Canonically, consider McKelvey's chaos theorem (1976). True, in some contexts, it may be possible to find stability in multidimensional policy environments (Shepsle 1979). The key point, though, is that absent some mechanism to reduce the dimensionality of the policy space, multidimensionality poses considerable challenges, both for the analyst and the analysis.

[6] A fascinating property of partisan unidimensionality is that parties can, and not uncommonly, have traded positions on salient issues yet maintained the image of ideological coherence across issues in general. See Karol (2009) for a fascinating account of the politics of changes in the parties' policy positions.

ity of the alternatives across the wide array of specific policies on offer to voters. And of still more interest (to us, certainly), and again agreed across-the-board, political parties provide a causal mechanism allowing voters to recognize programmatic coordination across diverse policy domains. What is that mechanism? The policy reputations of the parties.

We wish to emphasize that there is nothing original in proposing a theory centered on the concept of parties' having policy reputations. The theoretical foundations for the concept of party policy reputations or brand names were first laid in the study of congressional parties. The idea of party policy reputations has since been formally extended to the analysis of voting in partisan elections and legislative accountability. What is more, for at least a generation, behaviorally oriented political scientists have been demonstrating that partisans are more likely to favor a candidate or policy of their party if the candidate or policy is party-branded.

There is no modesty, false or otherwise, in our saying there is nothing original in our use of the concept of party policy reputations. Our objective has been to build on the work of others in order to use what is now known to learn what is not yet known. And, for all the use of the concept of policy reputations, there is a puzzle about reputational effects. There is no question that partisans are more likely to favor policies of their party if the brand name of their party is attached to them. But why the need to attach the brand name of the party to the policy? If the parties have indeed stamped their brand on a policy, it should not be necessary continually to remind their supporters of their party's position.

A party has a policy reputation just so far as people have taken on board what it stands for. The key to a reputational effect, it follows, is precisely that a reminder is not necessary. This may seem a merely negative point. It is a pivotal point. In previous research, proof of a reputational effect has been observing more support for a policy or candidate in response to a party cue. From our perspective, the point is precisely that they don't need to be cued. It is the superfluousness of reminders that is evidence of a reputational effect. Need we add that our argument is not that the concept of a "reputational effect" can mean only one thing, and the one thing it means is what we assert it means? It is rather that in advancing a reputational theory of spatial reasoning, we aim to bring out a neglected meaning of the idea of parties' having a reputation.

Having touted some advantages of our supply-side focus on political parties and the consistency of electoral choice, we are loath to conclude this section without repeating a warning about the limits of our theory. They include, *inter alia*: having nothing to say about political independents; abstentions; primaries; its greater relevance in some political eras (i.e., polarized ones), its lesser relevance in others (i.e., ideologically moderate ones).

A PARADOX: CITIZEN COMPETENCE AND PARTISAN REPUTATION

We have aimed to develop and test a reputational theory of party identification and party-centered spatial reasoning. We want to conclude by bringing out the double-edged implication of our theory and findings for the vexed issue of citizen competence.

Viewed at one level, our findings demonstrate that substantial numbers in the electorate can and do make politically consistent, indeed, ideologically coherent, choices over candidates and policies. And the theory we advance identifies the mechanisms by which they do so, the conjunction of motives that they need to do so, and the specific piece of knowledge they require to do so. This is a claim of a higher degree of political competence of voters (assuming that it holds up under critical scrutiny) than the entrenched image in public opinion research that citizens are empty-headed (the non-attitudes problem) or muddle-headed (the lack of constraint problem);[7] or just "make it up as they go along";[8] or that describing their thinking as "casual and shallow" would be excessive praise.[9]

To be clear, we offer this claim of citizen competence in the spirit of a memorable quip of the distinguished English historian, A.J.P. Taylor. In response to the president of Corpus College saying, "I hear you have strong political views," A.J.P. Taylor, the English historian replied, "Oh

[7] The most intellectually arresting exposition of this view of mass belief systems remains Converse's (1964) depiction of mass belief systems.

[8] "Making it up as you go along" is the title of chapter 5 in Zaller (1992). For a detailed critique of Zaller's "making it up" thesis, see Sniderman, Tetlock, and Elms (2001).

[9] Bartels (2003), 63. The test strictly is context-independent choice which Bartels rules out on the grounds of the limits of natural language and the architecture of the brain. His claim of an inherent inability to achieve consistency thus has nothing particularly to do with politics (55).

no, President, extreme views, weakly held."[10] Relative to many of the claims in the public opinion research, ours are extreme with respect to the outcome—consistency of choice—but they are modest with respect to citizens' role in the choice process. We quite agree that citizens do not have the resources to achieve a level of political coherence on their own. Political institutions do the heavy lifting for them, reducing, coordinating, labeling, and advertising the alternatives on offer.

Voters who know and share the outlook of their party are more competent to make policy-consistent choices, we contend. But ours is far from a story of democratic triumphalism. Consider the implications of the two principal components of our theory—a reputational premium and the Order Rule for the electoral logic of candidate positioning.

Figure 5.1 picks out four positions that a Democratic candidate may take relative to a Republican moderate.

D_1 and D_2 take positions straightforwardly consistent with the policy reputation of the Democratic Party, albeit in different senses. By the standard of legislative voting, D_1's liberal position is the most consistent with the Democratic Party's programmatic orientation in a politically polarized era. On the other hand, on an everyday understanding of the relationship "consistent with," D_2 stands with the program of the Democratic Party, to the left of the midpoint (M). In contrast, the position of D_3 is conservative, modestly so but all the same distinctively so, while the position of D_4 is extremely conservative, lining up at the far right pole.

On the ordinary understanding of "consistent with," D_3 and D_4 have taken positions at variance with the program of their party. The electoral logic of candidate positioning provides an incentive for Democratic candidates to line up at any point to the left of the center point, the liberal side, and to shun any position to the right of the center point. Follow this rule, and they will get the full benefit of a reputational premium. The Order Rule generates a different logic of candidate positioning, however. A Democratic candidate collects a reputational premium, and what is more, collects it in full, if he takes up a position at any point to the left of R, the Republican candidate. In the hypothetical set of scenarios in figure 5.1, this means that D_3, as well as D_1 and D_2, collect premium support from their party's supporters who know and share the outlook of their

[10] Taylor (1983), 56.

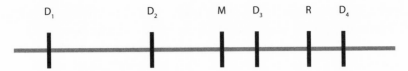

Figure 5.1: The Latitude Prediction

party. We have termed this the Latitude Prediction, and it follows from the two principal components of our theory—a reputational premium and the Order Rule.

The Latitude Prediction is a radical claim, we recognize. If D_1, D_2, *and* D_3 are equivalent positions, then a Democratic candidate can position himself anywhere between D_1 *and* D_3, conditional on running against a moderately conservative Republican, and still be awarded a reputational premium. Since he will in any case have the backing of traditional partisans, this is tantamount to saying that he can choose any point to the left of his opponent, yet collect from his camp the fullest measure of support from strong partisans who know and share the outlook of their party. We acknowledge that this claim violates the commonsense understanding of what it means for candidates to take positions consistent with the political outlook of their party. But common sense should not be dispositive.

For many years, political scientists took it as axiomatic that candidates lost support if they moved to the political extremes because they were moving away from the political preferences of the average (or more exactly, median) voters.[11] But the reality of American politics is at odds with arguably the all-in-all most elegant theory of politics.[12] That is, we believe, just where our findings make a contribution, and not by challenging the candidate-centered Downsian model but instead by supplementing it.

Contemporary American politics is distinguished by the conjunction of two features. Party elites are polarized. Republican politicians are not merely conservative; they are very conservative. Democratic politicians are not merely liberal; they are very liberal. But there is a disconnect be-

[11] This claim holds on the assumption that the median voter is herself not at the extremes—reasonably enough.

[12] It does not follow that the median voter theorem is wrong. As we have noted, there is no shortage of explanations to account for this disconnect between theory and reality—the disproportionate influence of more extreme partisans in primaries; the power of money and interest groups; the pull of political activists, among them.

tween party leaders and their supporters.[13] While party leaders are polarized, party supporters are sorted but not polarized. Republican supporters are conservative but they are moderate conservatives and not necessarily conservative on all issues. Democratic supporters are liberal; but they are moderate liberals and by no means liberal on all issues. What is more, it is not just that party candidates can take extreme positions without being punished by a loss of support. Despite this disconnect, candidates who line up at the poles collect a full reputational premium.

It is one thing when party leaders get away with taking extreme positions because they fly under the cognitive radar of less sophisticated supporters of their party. It is another thing when they can do so with party supporters who know and share the outlook of their party. And it is not only that they are not punishing their party's candidates for taking extreme stands. They are rewarding them. True, to get this bonus support candidates must satisfy the minimal condition of being on the appropriate ideological side of the candidate of the opposing party. But this threshold condition is no more than an inch off the ground in an era of polarized politics. And it is not as though these party supporters are hornswoggled.[14] Though they themselves tend to be moderate, they know that their party is near the ideological pole.[15]

This disconnect—extreme representatives, moderate supporters within both parties[16]—points to a paradox. Understanding of the ideological logic of the party system as well as ignorance of it loosens the power of party supporters to tie the (policy) hands of their leaders. And what makes this all the more curious is that the politically sophisticated supporters are

[13] In choosing the term "disconnect," we mean to flag that we are following the lead of Morris P. Fiorina (see Fiorina and Abrams, 2009). His comparative focus is different from ours in a key respect, though. We compare preferences of partisan elites with those of party supporters. He compares preferences of partisan elites with those of the electorate as a whole. Hence the difference between the shapes of ours and his preference curves for voters. His are unimodal, since the electorate includes independents as well as party identifiers. Ours are bimodal, since the comparison is between party elites and (largely sorted) party supporters.

[14] We thank our colleague, Jonathan Wand, for bringing this critical issue to our attention.

[15] Over the last decade, Republicans who know and share the outlook of their party place it at about 5.7 on the NES liberal-conservative scale, while locating the Democratic Party at around 2.1. Their Democratic counterparts locate their party at around 2.6, while placing the Republicans at about 6.16. In particular, programmatic Republicans placed the Republican Party at 5.6, 5.7, and 5.7 in the 2000, 2004, and 2008 NES surveys, respectively; the corresponding figures for the placement of the Democratic party were 2.2, 2.1, and 1.9.

[16] Yes, we are aware of the Tea Party.

doing the right thing for the right reason—on any reasonable definition of right. True, programmatic partisans are not better off voting for the candidate of their party in all conceivable circumstances. And our findings show that they attach as much weight to the positions of the candidates as other voters.[17] But in the world of American politics as it is, for party supporters to put their money on the policy reputations of the parties is the best rule for them to follow. And best in a triple sense. Choosing on the basis of the parties' reputations is the easiest rule to follow, requiring the lowest information cost since party reputations are widely diffused and highly salient. Furthermore, party reputations are not only the lowest cost but also the most reliable signal. The policy reputations of the parties are a better predictor of the package of legislative outcomes than the particular policy positions of candidates sponsored by the two parties. And finally, since the policy bundles that the parties offer represent the closest match to the overall outlooks of party identifiers who understand and are in sync with the ideological logic of the party, party reputations are the best guide to realizing their preferences all in all. Programmatic partisans are thus making their best bet, taking into account the information that is available and the institutional realities.

Ours is a limited theory of candidate positioning. It specifies the range of positions that party candidates may take and collect a reputational premium. It identifies the mechanisms that open the door for them to take more extreme positions than the supporters of their party without suffering an electoral penalty. But it does not—and as a purely voter-centered theory cannot—identify the incentives that induce party representatives to take more polarized positions than their supporters.[18] What our party-centered theory of spatial reasoning contributes that candidate-centered theories do not is an account of how political sophistication increases

---

[17] This is evident in several places in our account, but perhaps most clearly in table 4.6, where we see that the coefficient on spatial proximity is actually higher for programmatic partisans than traditional partisans. Thus, if anything, programmatic partisans in fact exhibit greater levels of Downsian competence than traditional partisans.

[18] As we have suggested, representatives may adopt relatively extreme positions for a variety of reasons: pressure from interest groups; or from party bosses, for example. Or perhaps the primary electorate, populated as it is with extremists, induces candidates to adopt off-center positions; or perhaps, quite apart from strategic positioning, the primary system drives away moderate candidates from running for office in the first place. Here, we only suggest several arguments, and leave the task of adjudicating between these possibilities—and countless others—to other scholars.

the latitude of positions that party leaders may take without electoral punishment.

CODA

An ever-recurring theme of the study of public opinion has been the ways that citizens fall short of the ideals of democratic citizenship. It is as though things would have gone well, or at any rate much better, but for them; as though the policy of the day would have been wiser, or its implementation more principled or efficient, but for their paying too little attention to public affairs. No doubt right sometimes, though as a general principle not self-evidently so. Yet, there is no way of getting round the immense mountain of evidence documenting how little citizens know about politics and how little attention they pay it. Ignorance exacts a price, and part of the price of voters' ignorance of politics and public affairs surely has been the imperfect realization of democratic values.

The focus of this study, however, has not been the politically ill-informed and detached. It instead has been their fellow citizens who do all that can reasonably be expected of a citizen. They form large and coherent views of politics. They understand the ideological logic of the American party system. They support the party that represents their outlook. And what is the consequence? In the contemporary era of American politics, citizens who more nearly approach the standards of democratic citizenship free up their elected representatives to take extreme positions. If true, this is an unhappy conclusion from the point of view of democratic theory. Then again, the happiness (or lack of it) of a conclusion has nothing to do with its empirical validity.

A Limit on the Influence of the Policy Reputations of Parties

THE PIVOTAL MECHANISM of our theory of party identification and party-centered spatial reasoning is the policy reputations of the political parties. Their reputations serve as a signal, activating party-centered reasoning. In the process, they broadly constrain how candidates running under their opposing banners must align themselves vis-à-vis one another in order to collect a reputational premium from partisans who know and share the outlook of their party. Through multiple experiments in multiple studies, we have provided evidence of the importance of the parties' policy reputations. We recognize that we could now say, job done: all the evidence of their importance is on the table for colleagues to evaluate. But we believe that one part of the job remains to be done. The task of a theory is to identify the conditions under which critical variables are consequential and the conditions under which they are not. We have identified conditions under which policy reputations of the party influence spatial reasoning. We now want to take one more step and specify the limits of their influence on spatial reasoning.

INTRODUCTION

Since the early 1970s, political elites—most notably, elected representatives in Congress—have diverged ideologically on partisan lines. In recent Congresses, Republican representatives almost exclusively hold conservative political views, and what is more, very conservative views at that. Similarly, Democratic representatives almost exclusively hold liberal political views, and quite liberal views at that, if possibly not as liberal as their Republican counterparts are conservatives. This possible nuance aside, observers agree that both parties have become less centrist or moderate, more extremist or polarized. The causes and consequences of ideological divergence over the last thirty years or so are disputed, it is only fair to add. But so far as the simple empirical fact of elite-level polarization is concerned, researchers are singing from the same hymn sheet (see, e.g., McCarty, Poole, and Rosenthal 2006).[1]

Our focus is ordinary citizens, not political activists, and if there is a chorus of agreement about partisan elites, there is a cacophony of views about the electorate. Some take the position that the general public is as moderate in its views now as it was a generation ago.[2] Others take the position that Americans have become divided into opposing camps. "Red" states versus "Blue" states is one metaphor, the "culture wars" another, the popularity of these images itself evidence of the wide currency of the notion of polarization.[3]

This dispute about the fact of polarization at the level of the public at large is, at least in part, a function of the different meanings assigned to the concept of polarization. Sometimes, the concept refers to the distance between the policy preferences of the median supporters of the two parties.[4] Other times, it designates the extremity of evaluative responses to political leaders.[5] Still other times, polarization is shorthand for the emotional heat of issues, particularly on the "traditional values" agenda, a prototypical example being the issue of abortion.[6] And still other times, polarization refers to the consistency with which partisans back the policies of their party.[7] To be fair, there is nothing exceptional about the abundance of meanings attached to the concept of polarization. Political science terms seem to invite definitional promiscuity.[8]

---

[1] However, several scholars have suggested that elite-level polarization is over-stated. Theriault (2006), for example, argues that the composition of the legislative agenda amplifies the level of polarization evident in the congressional roll call record. Stiglitz and Weingast (2010), likewise, suggest that vote-buying and other common forms of parliamentary interaction can cause the roll call record to over-state the level of disagreement between members of the two parties.

[2] See, for example, Dimaggio, Evans, and Bryson (1996); Evans (2003); Fiorina, Abrams, and Pope (2005); Fiorina and Levendusky (2006).

[3] Abramowtiz and Sanders (2005); Jacobson (2005).

[4] Fiorina, Abrams, and Pope (2005); Fiorina and Levendusky (2006).

[5] For example, Jacobson (2007).

[6] Hetherington and Weiler (2009).

[7] So defined, polarization is a synonym for sorting. See Levendusky (2009a, 2009b).

[8] Part of the difficulty, we believe, is that much of the scholarly literature discusses the topic as though the electorate either is or is not polarized, suggesting a simple dichotomous world (as in, analogously, a woman either is or is not pregnant). Instead, we believe it is use-

Then again, there is all the difference between a concept being put to different uses in research and researchers being confused about its use. The occasional exception notwithstanding, those who do work on polarization in mass politics are admirably up-front about just what job they are asking the concept of polarization to do. And they usually have good reason to use it as they do, we would add. Hetherington and Weiler (2009), to cite one example only, point to the anger/outrage that fuels arguments over issues such as gay marriage and abortion on the traditional values agenda. It thus is not necessary to be dogmatic about the meaning of polarization, only clear.

Ours is a study of spatial reasoning, so the sense in which we understand policy polarization is spatial. Preferences are distributed along a policy dimension, characteristically running from left to right. When a high proportion of citizens within one party locate near a pole and a high proportion of citizens in the opposing party locate near the opposing pole, the electorate is more polarized. By contrast, when a high proportion of citizens from both parties locate near the center point, the distribution is less polarized. So defined, to claim that ordinary Americans are more polarized now than thirty years ago is to claim that decisively more now hold extreme positions across political parties—that is, are near the poles—while decisively fewer hold moderate positions—that is, are near the center point.

The evidence is one-sided on polarization, so conceived. For example, the aggregate proportions classifying themselves into various ideological categories (e.g., extremely liberal, liberal, and so on), plotted over time, reproduce the flat lines on a cardiac monitor of a patient who has suffered a fatal heart attack.[9] For that matter, the percentage variation in positions over four intervals from 1984 to 2004 on issues central to American political debate—health insurance, spending/services, aid to blacks, defense spending—are miniscule, typically on the order of only several percentage points—no more than muscle twitches, to continue the medical analogy.[10]

---

ful to think of polarization as a matter of degrees. This, at least, avoids the issue of forcing scholars to agree on an arbitrary threshold before which the electorate is unpolarized and beyond which it is polarized. Of course, even this issue aside, the difficulty of scholars using different data sets and different measures persists.

[9] Admittedly, figure 4 (Fiorina and Abrams 2008, 571) is an especially dramatic example, but not a misleading one all the same.

[10] Fiorina, Abrams, and Pope (2005).

It is possible to look at the problem of polarization in a quite different light, however, if one considers the dynamic of elite mobilization. Most of the time, citizens are caught up in the routines of life—family, work, their circle of friends, and social activities. It is only during the election season, and, most research shows, primarily during the last weeks of a campaign, that citizens engage with the issues of the day. It is in this brief stretch—an instant, by the measure of a congressional or presidential election cycle— that candidates and parties galvanize their supporters and spark them to see the choices before them in the light of their underlying predispositions, their partisan identifications very much among them.[11]

This "activation" model of campaigns carries an implication for a theory of polarization. Rather than conceiving of polarization as an enduring change of positions from moderate to extremist, it can be understood as a short-term spike. In this conception, in the weeks before an election or in a moment of political crisis—*that is to say, when it counts*—partisan elites can induce partisan identifiers to follow their lead in the heat of the moment and support more polarized positions than they would ordinarily.

Our objective is to throw light on the susceptibility of party identifiers to manipulation. Specifically, our aim is to determine whether party leaders can use their parties' policy reputations to induce their followers to adopt more extreme positions, even if only for a moment. In this sense, we investigate a different side of parties' policy reputations than we studied in the main portion of our project. There, we considered whether, for a subset of partisans, parties' policy reputations help voters realize their policy preferences, all in all; whether, for these voters, their parties' policy commitments represented a central element of their party identification. Here, by contrast, we consider whether parties can actually shape, over a short period, the positions that voters come to view as their own.

Our hypothesis is that parties-in-government can *not* induce the parties-in-the-electorate to adopt more extreme positions, even in the very short run and even under the most favorable circumstances. Our strategy is to use experimental interventions to pressure party identifiers to adopt more polarized positions to show that, whatever we do, we can barely budge them.

This may seem a wrong-footed approach. Nearly without exception, and for perfectly good reasons, experiments in political science are run

[11] Gelman and King (1993); Alvarez (1998).

to test the hypothesis that an experimental intervention will make a difference. We want to turn things the other way around, and show that we cannot make a difference, try as we will. In the process, the weaknesses of survey experiments that skeptics rightly observe—the fact that respondents represent a captive audience, for example—turn into strengths. If everything is working in favor of inducing respondents to move to more extreme positions—even for a millisecond—yet we can barely get them to twitch (cognitively speaking), the claim that they cannot be moved in real life is all the stronger.

We shall be arguing, then, against the view that party leaders can induce party identifiers to move from centrist to extreme positions. In particular, we argue that when party leaders adopt extreme positions, partisans do not follow them to the poles. Perhaps the best introduction to our argument is to set out its strongest competitor. Ordinary citizens, on a once standard view of public opinion, have only a hazy idea of where they stand on political issues. They may know whether they are for or against, but even then, on one admittedly extreme view, they "answer the question on the basis of whatever considerations are accessible 'at the top of the head.' "[12] On this view, when party supporters learn where their party is—in a survey experiment, for example—they carry on an internal monologue, as it were, saying to themselves, "Well, if that is where the Democratic (Republican) Party is, since I am a Democrat (Republican), that is where I must be, too." We might christen this the "tag-along" theory of public opinion, if we were being unkind. It is a nihilistic view, by any standard.

The nihilism, in fact, involves a double-negative. Partisans neither know where their party is, nor where they themselves are. We propose to take up each negative in turn.

REPUTATIONS AS ENCODED INFORMATION

How do parties shape the views of their supporters? For many years, the emphasis was on the role of parties as reference groups.[13] Their supporters are emotionally attached to the party, and by virtue of this attachment,

---

[12] Zaller (1992), 49.
[13] See, e.g., Jacoby (1991).

are inclined to adopt the views associated with their party. This could, though it need not, mean that emotional loyalty underwrote mindless conformity. A reformist clause was added, accordingly, picking out the role of political sophistication (Zaller 1992). An obvious precondition of following the lead of party leaders is being aware of the positions that they take. It follows that it is the most politically sophisticated who are the most likely to use parties as reference groups. Then, in the most recent wave of research, the role of parties' policy reputations has been brought to the fore.

The introduction of the concept of policy reputations has been a valuable addition on the plus side of the theoretical ledger. But a clause in the fine print has not received the full attention it deserves. Consider this thought experiment. The subject is the founding of a philanthropy. Branding consists in connecting a unique trademark and a distinctive product.

To take an example from life, we construct a visual and symbolic trademark, CoachArt, and a "product," providing underprivileged children and adolescents with chronic and life-threatening illnesses free, personal lessons in the arts and athletics.[14] Distinctiveness is the first requirement of both the trademark and product; and definiteness and durability of the connection between the two are the second and third requirements. If you have to remind people what a brand name stands for, you have failed to establish it.

How does this apply to parties as brand names? The policy reputations of the parties have "relatively precise meanings," James Snyder and Michael Ting contend. "Democratic candidates tend to be liberal, and Republicans tend to be conservative."[15] But what, more exactly, does it mean to say that parties have a policy reputation?[16] What is it that we are supposing that partisans who know the parties' policy reputations actually know when they know that one set of players is liberal and their opponents conservative? Not liberalism and conservatism as political

---

[14] Coach Art was founded by Zander Lurie in honor of his father, Dr. Arthur Lurie, a distinguished cardiac surgeon. See CoachArt.org.

[15] Snyder and Ting (2002).

[16] Special-purpose terms enjoy fashion cycles. Party "images" was once in vogue. Party "reputations" has taken its place. The two are vehicles for a common premise—namely, that political parties (not just prominent figures) are a focal point for the electorates' evaluative judgments. The two terms also cover a lot of the same conceptual terrain, though reputation is narrower than image and more explicit in grounding the identity of political parties in their policy commitments. Since our concern is policy, we shall stick to reputation.

philosophies. We accept the portrait of citizens at large as only intermittently interested in politics. But if liberal and conservative do not refer to abstract political ideas, what do they refer to?

The concept of brand names carries on its back the metaphor of branding—as in cattle being branded. So conceived, the Democratic Party stamps a liberal brand on its policy products, the Republican Party a conservative brand on its own. This metaphor of branding a policy does more conceptual work than commonly recognized, we believe. To brand a policy is to affix a marker. To say that parties brand their policies is thus to say that the policies are identified with the parties, in the minds of those who know the policy reputations of the parties. And to say this is to say that a party's policies bear its mark even without its label having to be attached to them on each and every occasion.

Let us walk (slightly) uphill with this line of argument. If the parties have successfully established policy reputations, then a reference to the policies that the party is associated with should be exchangeable with a reference to the party itself. In turn, partisans who know the ideological ordering of the parties—that is, know their policy reputations—should be able accurately to locate candidates on the broad dimension of liberalism-conservatism solely on the basis of the candidate's party affiliation. And, to take the last step in this inferential parade, at least with respect to policies associated with a party, attaching a party label to the policies should be superfluous. In short, a political party has a policy reputation just so far as people have taken on board the positions and general point of view it stands for—in the parlance, they have encoded the information.

The Stickiness of Preferences

Our second premise is the stickiness of preferences. It may sound odd to speak of political preferences as sticky. The discovery of non-attitudes triggered a skepticism avalanche as to whether, when it comes to public opinion, there is any there. In the most influential formulation of its time, the rallying cry was that "most people, on most issues, do not 'really think' any particular thing."[17] The initial wave of "framing" experiments

[17] Zaller (1992), 194. The quote is not an isolated one. Other formulations include that "*most* people really aren't sure what their opinions are on *most* political matters"; p. 76,

further reinforced the scholarly sense of the vacuousness of public opinion.[18] In the mantra of the day, whoever controlled the framing of an issue controlled the side that the majority would favor. Smart money bet against citizens knowing where they stood on the issues of the day. They might say that they had a position on an issue. But likely as not, that was to cloak the fact that they had not taken the trouble to form one. So, even in the absence of substantive arguments or interpersonal influence, they would float from one side of an issue to the other, then back again, carried back and forth by chance and circumstance. In contrast, a premise of our approach is that policy preferences are sticky.

This is not theoretical self-pleading. The use of the concept of non-attitudes as a launching point for a theory of public opinion owed its plausibility to its abstractness, some would say, others to the brilliance of its scientific launch by Converse. But short shrift would have been made of any political scientist who stepped forward to claim that Americans decided by a flip of the coin whether they supported or opposed racial quotas, or wanted to legalize gay marriages or not, or favored "reform" of welfare, or had a preference about whether their taxes should be increased or not. On all these and many other issues, citizens have preferences—definite, often strong, usually strongly felt.

And so their preferences accordingly are sticky. To characterize preferences as sticky is of course to make a claim about their stability, or still more strongly, their resistance to change. Stability (or resistance to change) is a matter of degree. Some preferences are fleeting; some durable. Here, our concern is with partisans' preferences about issues that parties contest on a regular basis—to name a few: the issue of individual responsibility versus government assistance; gun control; environmental regulation; foreign policy that makes use of military force; government assistance for blacks.[19] We have some direct evidence on the stickiness

---

italics added for emphasis; indeed, that most of the people, most of the time, just "make it up as they go along."

[18] E.g., Nelson and Kinder (1996); Zaller (1992).

[19] The questions are, respectively: (1) Which position is closer to what you think? The federal government should make every effort to ensure that everybody has a good standard of living OR Each individual has a responsibility to get ahead on their own. (2) Which position is closer to what you think? Government should make it more difficult to buy guns OR The rules should be about the same as they are now. (3) Which is closer to what you believe? We need tougher government regulations on business OR Current regulations to protect the environment are already. (4) Which is closer to your view? The United States has the right to

of preferences on this roll call of issues, conditional on the method of measurement and mode of interview in our studies. In a panel study with Wave 1 and 2 interviews modally separated by four and a half months, the median stability coefficient is 0.72, the range, 0.65 to 0.75.[20]

There is a deeper issue, though, flagged by the phrase "conditional on method of measurement and mode of interview." Stability coefficients are not part of the furniture of the world. What we observe when we measure the stability of attitudinal responses over time is tied to the mode of measurement.[21] This may seem no more than an ordinary Sunday sermon on the theory of measurement, but for reasons that have more to do with a desire to lower study costs than to increase scientific rigor, the practice has been to calculate stability coefficients with the least ambitious technology—single indicator measures, often with self-assigned locations on a multi-point scale rather than branching formats.[22] This approach to measurement often produces low stability coefficients. In contrast, using multiple indicators, Ansolabehere, Rodden, and Snyder (2008) show that a large family of attitudinal constructs exhibit comparable degrees of stability over two- and four-year intervals as American political behavior's flagship measure—party identification.

Preferences on issues the parties contest are sticky, we conclude, and so are party reputations. These are premises. They point, in turn, to two lines of reasoning. The first has to do with partisans who have definite policy views and know their way about the political landscape. All would agree, they should not be easily goaded or gulled into taking a more extreme or immoderate position than they ordinarily would. The second has to do with classical partisans. They should be similarly difficult to polarize, albeit for quite different reasons. They are out-of-step with their party's program, yet as party loyalists, are reluctant to believe their party rejects their beliefs. And just so far as they believe their party is centrist, it should be difficult to induce traditional Democrats to take extreme liberal

---

attack any country it thinks might attack the United States OR The United States should not attack another country unless that country has attacked the United States first. (5) Which position is closer to what you think? Government should make a stronger effort to improve the position of blacks OR Blacks should take responsibility for helping themselves.

[20] We follow standard measurement techniques by examining the correlation coefficient between responses to the same item in surveys conducted at points in time.

[21] For the original presentation of this argument, see Achen (1975).

[22] E.g., Malhotra, Krosnick, and Thomas (2009).

positions, or traditional Republicans to embrace extreme conservative ones, under the banner of supporting their party's programs.

CAN PARTIES INDUCE POLARIZATION SPIKES?

It is our hypothesis that, even under the most favorable conditions, parties have a very limited ability to induce policy moderates to take extreme positions. In three ways, we have designed the Polarization Experiment to work against our hypothesis.

For one thing, the standard NES policy scale has 7 points, with 4 as the neutral point. The small number of units—7—limits our ability to observe the consequences of party reputations. A respondent's underlying policy views may move toward the poles after a party "treatment," though her response to the 7-point scale remains unaltered because of the lumpiness of the response format. So we have put in place an 11-point scale. The extra length should make it as easy as possible for respondents to slide in the direction of policy poles in response to a partisan or ideological political signal, even if they still are not inclined to go all the way. The more granular response format thus allows us to detect even small polarization effects.

Our second design decision concerned the multiplication of signals. In the baseline condition of the Polarization Experiment, policies are introduced in the standard neutral style: "Some people . . . Other people. . . . In the three other conditions, the introductory phrase is respectively: "Democrats think . . . Republicans think . . ."; and "Very liberal people think . . . Very conservative people think." In principle, either of the political signals, party or ideology, can induce a polarization effect. But to be on the side of the (experimental) angels, we added a fourth condition, combining the two signals: "Very liberal Democrats . . . Very liberal Republicans . . ." Better to hit them on the head too hard, we reasoned, than to fail to catch their attention at all.

The first two of our design features are apple pie. The third is well out of the mainstream, we confess. We first carried out the Polarization Experiment with 1,023 respondents. Failing to find a significant effect, yet noticing the bare glimmering of a pattern, we enlarged the sample. Drive down the standard errors by increasing the number of respondents, we reasoned. So we conducted the experiment with another 1,534 respondents, and since they were randomly selected like the first 1,000 respondents, we pooled two samples and redid the analysis. Again failing to find a significant effect, yet still noticing a pattern, we interviewed a third tranche of respondents, boosting the final sample size up to 3,609.[23]

This repeated sampling and pooling of respondents in an experiment is an outside-the-box procedure, we acknowledge. But we did it to counteract a stereotype about scientific experiments.[24] Experiments are designed to induce an effect, most suppose. If responses in the "treatment" condition fail to differ significantly from those in the control condition, their under-their-breath presumption is that the experiment has failed. The fault is with its design—too little statistical power to detect too weak an experimental manipulation. If the manipulation fails to show results, we do not want this null result to stem from our design.

Our substantive hypothesis, after all, is that even under favorable circumstances, partisans cannot be induced to take up more extreme positions than they otherwise would. So we have done all in our power to reject this hypothesis—increasing sample size, and then increasing it yet again. And we shall show that, with sufficient resources, coupled with sufficiently adroit restrictions on statistical analyses, treatment effects can approach or reach standard levels of statistical significance. But the sheer extravagance of this effort reinforces our theoretical claim: even under the most favorable circumstances and in the heat of the moment, "polarization" effects are trivial.

Table A.1 reports the responses of programmatic and traditional partisans in our experimental settings.[25] The experimental conditions are arrayed, from left to right, in (approximate) order of the strength of the polarizing cue: on the far left is the baseline or no cue condition; on the far right the double cue; and in between, the two single cues. Each cell presents three pieces of information: mean score (scaled from −5, most liberal, to +5, most conservative); number of respondents, and importantly, standard errors.

[23] In the third tranche, only Democrats and Republicans were added to the sample, further increasing the efficiency of our estimates. See studies 7A, 7B, and 7C in appendix B.

[24] Sniderman (2011).

[25] To increase the number of cases in the table cells and decrease the number of cells, "traditional" and "mixed" partisans are combined.

Consider first the issue of medical and hospital costs. Two policy alternatives were presented: that a government insurance plan would cover all medical and hospital expenses for everyone, or that medical expenses should be paid by individuals through private insurance plans like Blue Cross. The wording for our question is borrowed from the National Election Study. Notice that the policy choices anchor the spatial poles, but they are not semantically characterized as "extreme" or "polar" positions in the question wording.

As table A.1 shows, even in the absence of a political cue, the parties distinctly diverge, Democrats taking a stand definitely on the liberal side (mean $= -1.83$), the Republicans as definite a stand on the conservative side (mean $= 1.47$). Visually, they appear to diverge more when either a partisan or ideological cue is paired with the policy alternatives, or when we combine both cues. Thus, the difference between the Democratic and Republican means in the combined party-ideology condition is approximately four and a half points, compared to about three points in the no cue condition. The difference is statistically significant. But it is substantively trivial.

The pattern for the issue of stem cell research is similar. Respondents were presented with two polar positions—". . . feel very strongly that the Federal government should fund stem cell research" and ". . . feel very strongly that the government should not fund stem cell research"—at opposite ends of an 11-point scale.[26] Note that partisans move toward their respective poles in the combined cue condition, compared to the no cue condition. More tellingly, note the minuscule distance that they move. For Democrats, from -1.81 in the no condition to -2.19 in the combined cue condition, and 0.98 and 1.45, for Republicans—again about a half-point, for both Democrats and Republicans, in opposing directions.

In addition to medical care and stem cell research, we also examined susceptibility to polarization for two other issues. One was immigration. Respondents were presented with two alternatives—do they think that "illegal immigrants should be allowed to stay here legally if they pay a fine and meet other requirements," versus do they believe that "illegal immigrants should be sent back to their native countries." The other issue was government assistance versus self-reliance. In this case, we ask

[26] Underlining in visual presentation of the test item.

TABLE A.1: *Weak Evidence of a Polarization Effect*

	Baseline		Ideology Cue		Party Cue		Party and Ideology Cues	
	Democrat	Republican	Democrat	Republican	Democrat	Republican	Democrat	Republican
Health Insurance	−1.83	1.47	−2.09	1.75	−2.36	1.86	−2.19	1.97
	(0.18)	(0.19)	(0.16)	(0.17)	(0.15)	(0.18)	(0.16)	(0.18)
	N=312	N=301	N=359	N=306	N=324	N=313	N=368	N=303
Stem Cell	−1.81	0.98	−2.14	0.9	−2.19	1.45	−1.93	1.03
	(0.19)	(0.21)	(0.17)	(0.21)	(0.18)	(0.19)	(0.17)	(0.21)
	N=312	N=301	N=359	N=305	N=323	N=313	N=366	N=303
Immigration	0.13	1.85	−0.04	2.29	−0.56	2.62	0.3	2.48
	(0.21)	(0.19)	(0.2)	(0.17)	(0.19)	(0.16)	(0.19)	(0.17)
	N=310	N=301	N=358	N=305	N=324	N=312	N=366	N=302
Government Assistance	−0.6	2.58	−0.98	2.39	−1.22	2.66	−1.33	2.8
	(0.19)	(0.15)	(0.16)	(0.16)	(0.16)	(0.15)	(0.16)	(0.15)
	N=311	N=302	N=359	N=304	N=324	N=314	=366	N=303

Note: Standard errors located below means in parentheses. The number of observations in each cell located below standard errors.

respondents to choose between whether they "feel the government should see to it that every person has a job and a good standard of living" versus "the government should let each person get ahead on their own." The results for the second two issues are consistent with those of the first two. On both issues, and for both parties, the means in the no cue condition coupled with the size of an 11-point scale leave ample room for respondents to move toward either pole without having to take the most extreme position possible. But once more the "polarization" effect is conspicuous for its modesty: again no more than a half a point for both Democrats and Republicans.

One response to these results is that we have not examined the most relevant group of citizens. In table A.1, we consider the influence of cues on *all* partisans—moderates and extremists alike. Given this sample, it is not surprising, a critic might retort, to find little evidence of polarization. Many of the partisans in the sample *already* possessed extremist views, and cues could not possibly have any influence on these citizens. Including these extremist partisans in the sample, the critic observes, pushes down the estimated polarization effect. The question of real interest to this critic is whether *moderates* alter their policy views on the basis of party and ideological cues.

This is a reasonable criticism. Accordingly, we recalculate table A.2, only this time focusing exclusively on ideological moderates. We exclude from the sample any respondent who self-identifies as "extremely liberal / conservative," and, for good measure, any respondent who self-identifies as a "liberal" or a "conservative." This leaves in our sample only "slightly" liberal and conservative citizens, and of course the self-identified moderates themselves. Table A.2 reports the results from this exercise. Notice that, sensibly, moderates—as determined by ideology self-identification— tend to have more moderate policy preferences.

The central observation from table A.2, however, is that moderate partisans behave no differently than the full sample of partisans. From the baseline condition to the "double-whammy" condition, Democrats move less than a half a point on the 11-point scale on the issue of medical insurance. Republicans polarize only slightly more substantially on the issue—by about three-quarters of a unit on the same scale. The results related to the other three issues, also reported in table A.2, corroborate

TABLE A.2: Weak Evidence of a Polarization Effect among Moderates

	Baseline		Ideology Cue		Party Cue		Party and Ideology Cues	
	Democrat	Republican	Democrat	Republican	Democrat	Republican	Democrat	Republican
Health Insurance	-1.46	0.24	-1.89	0.79	-2.07	0.68	-1.78	0.98
	(0.23)	(0.28)	(0.2)	(0.25)	(0.19)	(0.27)	(0.21)	(0.29)
	N=186	N=130	N=219	N=148	N=203	N=136	N=233	N=127
Stem Cell	-1.39	-0.44	-1.83	-0.52	-1.88	0.11	-1.63	-0.36
	(0.25)	(0.29)	(0.22)	(0.28)	(0.22)	(0.29)	(0.21)	(0.32)
	N=186	N=131	N=218	N=148	N=202	N=135	N=231	N=127
Immigration	0.63	1.15	0.3	1.61	0.17	2.18	1.03	1.63
	(0.26)	(0.3)	(0.26)	(0.25)	(0.24)	(0.26)	(0.23)	(0.3)
	N=185	N=131	N=217	N=148	N=203	N=134	N=232	N=126
Government Assistance	-0.36	1.62	-0.95	1.61	-0.97	1.47	-1.09	1.98
	(0.24)	(0.26)	(0.2)	(0.23)	(0.21)	(0.24)	(0.21)	(0.26)
	N=185	N=131	N=218	N=147	N=203	N=136	N=231	N=127

Note: Standard errors located below means in parentheses. The number of observations in each cell located below standard errors. Results based on subset of moderate respondents (slightly liberal, moderate, slightly conservative).

the fundamental conclusion that moderates do not polarize in response to political cues.

REPLICATION

The results of the Polarization Experiment suggest that party leaders have a limited capacity to induce their supporters to take more extreme issue stands through the manipulation of partisan or ideological signals. But it is only one experiment. And holes can be punched in any experiment by an advocate with a clever brief.

What has the "manipulation" actually consisted of in the Polarization Experiment? Merely attaching a label to a position, identifying it as the position of liberals (conservatives) or Democrats (Republicans), or attempting to deliver the strongest signal, very liberal Democrats (very conservative Republicans). But suppose someone is, and sees himself as being, a moderately liberal Democrat. Why should he necessarily feel impelled to take a more extreme stand on a policy than he ordinarily would because it is said to be the position of "very liberal Democrats"?

Policy labeling is the manipulation de jour in party branding experiments.[27] But affixing a label on a position is not the same thing as saying, "Here is where good Democrats (Republicans) stand on this issue. Come over here and stand with them." The partisan and ideological labels put to use in the Polarization Experiment are only implicitly spatial. To characterize a position as one held by a Democrat or by a very liberal Democrat is to locate a position on a policy continuum. But it is to do so only indirectly. Surely, more can and should be done in the way of giving directions, of indicating where as Democrats (Republicans) they should locate themselves.

There is also a strong case for replication. Doubtless, putting a hypothesis to a second independent test is always a good idea. But the need to do so here goes beyond methodological piety. Our argument is that attempts to induce partisans to take immoderate or polarized stands, even in the heat of the moment as it were, are likely to fail. But it is easy to dismiss failure of a manipulation in a survey experiment to produce a bankable

[27] e.g., Rahn (1993); Jacoby (1988); Squire and Smith (1988); Kam (2005); Merolla, Stephenson, and Zechmeister (2008).

result on the grounds that the manipulation was too weak. There are practical, not to mention ethical, constraints on what can be done in a public opinion interview, after all. And precisely because the failure of an experimental treatment to polarize preferences counts in favor of our hypothesis, we are under a special obligation to try again. Failing to find something counts as finding something only if one has done one's very best and still come away empty-handed.

So we conducted a second Polarization Experiment.[28] The backdrop idea was to put respondents in a position where they could, literally, picture where their party stood on an issue, to put them in the best possible position to say to themselves, well yes of course, as a Democrat (Republican) that is where I stand. In terms of experimental manipulations, the idea was to see how partisans respond to the movements of candidates. So the second experiment includes four conditions: (i) both parties take moderate positions; (ii) the Democratic Party takes an extremely liberal position while the Republican Party takes a moderately conservative one; (iii) the Democratic Party takes a moderately liberal position while the Republican Party takes an extremely conservative one; and (iv) both parties take extreme positions.

The use of the adverbs "moderately" and "extremely" deserves a word. On the one side, the objective is to have candidates take sharply contrasting positions; on the other side, the positions they take should be credible. So we ruled out self-defeatingly dramatic possibilities—say, positioning the Democratic candidate only a finger nail to the left of dead center while placing the Republican candidate to the right, as it were, of Louis XIV. So again we used a scale running from -5, the most liberal position, to 5, the most conservative. In the manipulations, we locate the Democratic Party either at a moderately liberal (-2) or a manifestly liberal (-4) position and the Republican Party at either a moderately conservative (2) or manifestly conservative (4) position.

Since replication is the goal, the second Polarization Experiment examines responses on two issues—immigration and stem cells—employed in the first—worded and formatted in the second just as in the first, naturally. And just as in the first Polarization Experiment, so in the second, after seeing where their party stands, partisans are asked where they them-

---

[28] See study 8, appendix B.

selves stand on the issues. Table A.3 shows the responses of Democratic and Republican Identifiers, first on the issue of immigration, then on the issue of stem cell research, in each of the four experimental conditions.

Consider the issue of immigration first. The Democratic Party finds its position a hard sell, even to its own supporters. In the baseline condition—when both parties have moderate positions—the mean position of Democratic identifiers is virtually dead center between the idea that immigrants who are living in the United States should be allowed to stay here legally if they pay a fine and meet other requirements, the liberal position, and that they should be sent back to their native countries, the conservative position. They are slightly more supportive of legalizing immigrants if either party takes a more extreme position, though the emphasis should be on the word "slightly." In the baseline condition, Democrats locate at an average of .06; when both parties take extreme positions, though one can see a movement to the left, it is no more than a twitch, the same half-point difference we saw in the maximum contrast in the first Polarization Experiment (mean $= -.55$).

The responses of Republican identifiers are dissimilar in one respect, but similar in another. The respect in which they are dissimilar is that they stand with their party on the policy of deporting illegal immigrants: in every experimental condition, they take an unambiguously conservative position, locating themselves on average in the neighborhood of 2. The respect in which Republican identifiers are similar to their Democratic counterparts is that, again between the maximum contrast conditions, Republican identifiers move a half-point to the right. This "change" is visually evident but not statistically let alone substantively significant.

The second issue is stem cell research. As the second panel in table A.3 shows, there is virtually no variation from one experimental condition to another. Democratic identifiers take a position on the left, though far from an extreme one; Republican identifiers take a position on the right, though not as far to the right as their Democratic counterparts take on the left. The parties do not have the power to goad, or gull, the ranks of their supporters to take extreme or immoderate positions on this issue, to judge from these results.

Here again, though, we confront the question of whether moderates respond to party cues—in this case, spatial cues—in the same way as partisans more generally. Consider the issue of immigration. When both

TABLE A.3: Weak Evidence of Polarization Effect with Spatial Cues

	Both Moderate		Democratic Moderate and Republican Extreme		Republican Moderate and Democratic Extreme		Both Extreme	
	Democrat	Republican	Democrat	Republican	Democrat	Republican	Democrat	Republican
Immigration	−0.06	2.29	−0.34	2.29	−0.25	2.1	−0.55	2.65
	(0.218)	(0.211)	(0.219)	(0.205)	(0.245)	(0.195)	(0.223)	(0.183)
	N=248	N=189	N=241	N=210	N=224	N=201	N=254	N=231
Stem Cell	−2.26	1.6	−2.23	1.18	−1.96	1.4	−1.89	1.13
	(0.197)	(0.241)	(0.186)	(0.227)	(0.209)	(0.235)	(0.195)	(0.225)
	N=247	N=189	N=240	N=211	N=226	N=202	N=254	N=229

Note: Standard errors located below means in parentheses. The number of observations in each cell located below standard errors.

TABLE A.4: Weak Evidence of Polarization Effect with Spatial Cues among Moderates

	Both Moderate		Democratic Moderate and Republican Extreme		Republican Moderate and Democratic Extreme		Both Extreme	
	Democrat	Republican	Democrat	Republican	Democrat	Republican	Democrat	Republican
Immigration	0.29	1.67	0.04	1.97	0.45	2.08	−0.37	2.26
	(0.28)	(0.33)	(0.27)	(0.35)	(0.31)	(0.31)	(0.28)	(0.3)
	N=147	N=82	N=153	N=79	N=140	N=76	N=159	N=97
Stem Cell	−1.55	0.27	−1.49	−0.31	−1.67	−0.24	−2.06	−0.17
	(0.23)	(0.41)	(0.26)	(0.4)	(0.26)	(0.31)	(0.26)	(0.35)
	N=159	N=75	N=134	N=78	N=142	N=95	N=167	N=86

Note: Standard errors located below means in parentheses. The number of observations in each cell located below standard errors. Results based on subset of moderate respondents (slightly liberal, moderate, slightly conservative).

parties locate in a moderate position, moderate Democrats express an average policy position of .29. If the parties locate at the extremes, moderate Democrats report an average policy preference of −.37. Similarly, moderate Republicans report an average immigration preference of 1.67 when the parties espouse moderate positions; this average preference increases to 2.26 when both parties adopt extreme positions. As evident in table A.4, the story is essentially the same for the issue of stem cell research. Thus, polarized parties induce movement in the preferences of moderate partisans—but, even for this group of partisans, the movement is modest. In all cases, the polarization effect is less than 1 point on an 11-point scale; generally, the polarization effect is less than one-half of one point on this scale.

In sum, the findings are all of one piece: whatever we have done, we have been unable to induce partisans to take more extreme positions to any substantively significant degree.

PRECIS

The possible polarization of American public opinion has been one of the most contested issues in the contemporary study of politics. Has the American electorate become more extreme, more immoderate in its political beliefs? To this point, the evidence brought to bear on this question has come from standard public opinion surveys. And rightly so. Trend studies tracking representative national cross-sectional samples provide the most direct answer to the question of polarization.

Though there are pluses and minuses in the evidentiary ledger, primarily because of the multiple uses of the concept of polarizations, we read the evidence as at odds with headline claims that ordinary Americans have become radically polarized across partisan lines. At least, if 1970 is the baseline, Americans, on average, appear to hold roughly the same views today as they did thirty years ago. All the same, they now form camps committed to opposing political programs under the banner of political parties in a way that they did not then, and at least part of the program—the so-called traditional values agenda—has the flavor of a culture war.

Still, as it looked to us, there was a key political possibility that had not been investigated. Even if one accepts the basic premise of an unpolarized electorate, though, this does not necessarily imply that the electorate is unpolarized in the heat of an election— *when it matters*. That is, the electorate can hold fundamentally centrist views for most of the time, but, like citizen-soldiers called to battle, partisans may take up the more polarized views of candidates or parties. This period just before decision day is no more than a historical moment, but what happens in this historical moment can define the politics of decades. We are not talking about party supporters becoming extremists, only their being willing to move somewhat nearer the polar positions that their parties hold, and then only moving for a moment, in the heat of a political argument, as it were.

Social scientists have been known to tout methodological remedies as substantive cure-alls. The introduction of survey experiments exploiting computer-assisted interviewing has arguably been the biggest methodological innovation in public opinion studies of politics in a half century. So, critical examination of the limits of survey experiments is a healthy development.[29]

For our part, the limits in carrying out survey experiments in public opinion interviews have always seemed the limits of good manners in everyday interchanges: consideration of the well-being of your guest and respect for the conventions of hospitality. True, the very fact that you are having a conversation and that you are assured that the other person is listening introduces a consideration that needs to be taken into account. In a survey experiment, the "treatment"—say, sharing some piece of information with the respondent— is designed to be immediately intelligible, and every respondent who is intended to receive it is guaranteed to receive it. By contrast, in real life, citizens tend to pay modest attention to politics and public affairs. So elite efforts at persuasion tend to pass them by, unnoticed.[30] Moreover, the dependent variables in experiments tend

[29] For the most searching examination of the limits of survey experiments as a method for the study of political belief, see Gaines, Kuklinski, and Quirk (2007). For a statement of the thesis that survey experiments can only—and should only—induce respondents to do what they already are predisposed to do, see Sniderman (2011).

[30] To our knowledge, Berelson, Lazarsfeld, and McPhee (1986) were the first to make the argument that citizen inattention to politics was a protective filter against elite manipulation. See also Zaller (1992).

to be sensitive—designed to detect even the most modest movements. In our context, respondents need only take a *somewhat* less centrist position for us to detect movement—and they need do so only for the length of time it takes for their fingers to strike a note on a piano keyboard. If partisan and ideological appeals cannot induce partisans to take more extreme positions in these unrealistically hospitable conditions, the only sensible conclusion is that this possibility is even more remote in the real political world.

A number of studies indicate that party leaders may be able to bring some supporters over the line to side with their party. But this is quite different from party leaders being able to induce their supporters to adopt less moderate positions in support of the party's program. They are unable to do so to any politically significant degree, our findings indicate. We believe that this unwillingness to give up moderate positions, even for just a moment and even in the face of direct partisan and ideological appeals, adds a new piece of evidence against the polarization claim. Yet, sometimes politics erupts, setting loose forces that overflow the boundaries of everyday expectations, and the drama of the choices that follow in their wake threatens to overwhelm us. Some times is not many times, to be sure. Then again, in politics extraordinary moments can have enduring effects. That party leaders cannot do much in the way of polarizing the preferences of their supporters during the regular season or even, possibly, the playoffs, that is as far as our findings go. What they can do at a critical moment in the political equivalent of the Super Bowl is another matter. Hence the relevance of our experimental findings on the inability of party leaders, even under extremely favorable conditions, to induce their supporters to take extreme or polarized positions.

Study Descriptions

GENERAL DESCRIPTION OF METHODOLOGY

DESCRIPTION OF KNOWLEDGEPANEL®

The Knowledge Networks (KN) Web panel is a probability-based panel. By definition, all members of the KN Web panel have a known probability of selection. As a result, it is mathematically possible to calculate a proper response rate that takes into account all sources of nonresponse. In contrast, opt-in Web panels do not permit the calculation of a response rate since the probabilities of selection are unknown. Consequently, opt-in panels are mathematically capable of computing only the survey completion rate representing the final stage of gaining cooperation of survey research subjects, excluding the nonresponse resulting from panel recruitment, connection, and panel retention.

The panel sample selection methodology used for this study was developed by KN in recognition of the practical issue that different surveys target different subpopulations. The methodology was also developed to attempt to correct for nonresponse and noncoverage error in the panel sample that could be introduced at the panel recruitment, connection, and panel retention stages of building and maintaining the panel.[1] The panel sample selection methodology, which has been used by KN since 2000,

---

[1] In K.N.'s patented solution (U.S. Patent No. 7,269,570), a survey assignment method uses a weighting factor to compensate for members which are temporarily removed from a panel because of an earlier draw of sample. This weighting factor adjusts the selection probabilities of the remaining panel members. The sample is drawn using systematic PPS sampling where the panel poststratification weights will be the Measures of Size (MOS). If the user requirements call for independent selection by stratum, the panel weights (MOS) are adjusted in the following procedure: Sum the MOS for each stratum, call this sum Sh for stratum h. Consider the user-specified or system-derived target sample size for stratum h to be nh. Then multiply each MOS for Members in stratum h by nh/Sh. Then use an interval of k = 1 and apply systematic PPS sampling to achieve the desired yield per stratum

provides statistical control on the representativeness of KN panel survey samples as measured by their proximity to population benchmarks.

STUDY ONE: Spatial Reasoning—Study One
Final Survey Completion Rates

Field Start Date	Field End Date	Number Fielded	Number Completed	Completion Rate	AAPOR RR3
10/11/02	12/31/02	12,054	9,313	77.3%	

Study Title: Political Opinion Survey

STUDY SEVEN 7A: Final Survey Completion Rates

Field Start Date	Field End Date	Number Fielded	Number Completed	Completion Rate	AAPOR RR3
10/17/07	10/31/07	1701	1280	75.2%	12.0%

7B: Final Survey Completion Rates

Field Start Date	Field End Date	Number Fielded	Number Completed	Completion Rate	AAPOR RR3
01/08/08	01/17/08	1412	1166	82.6%	12.6%

7C: Final Survey Completion Rates

Field Start Date	Field End Date	Number Fielded	Number Completed	Completion Rate	AAPOR RR3
09/11/07	09/28/07	1596	1222	76.6%	12.2%

7D: Final Survey Completion Rates

Field Start Date	Field End Date	Number Fielded	Number Completed	Completion Rate	AAPOR RR3
08/13/08	08/25/08	1657	1052	63.5%	7.7%

STUDY EIGHT: Final Survey Completion Rates

Field Start Date	Field End Date	Number Fielded	Number Completed	Completion Rate	AAPOR RR3
06/27/08	07/08/08	3216	2027	63.0%	9.1%

STUDY TEN: Final Survey Completion Rates

Field Start Date	Field End Date	Number Fielded	Number Completed	Completion Rate	AAPOR RR3
09/12/08	09/29/08	2496	1501	60.1%	7.3%

STUDY ELEVEN: Wave 11
Final Survey Completion Rates

Field Start Date	Field End Date	Number Fielded	Number Completed	Completion Rate	AAPOR RR3
12/16/08	12/28/08	4920	3378	68.7%	8.8%

References

Abramowitz, Alan I., and Kyle L. Saunders. 2005. "Is Polarization a Myth?" *Journal of Politics* 70: 542–555.

———. 2006. "Exploring the Bases of Partisanship in the American Electorate: Social Identity vs. Ideology." *Political Research Quarterly* 59: 175–187.

Achen, Christopher. 1975. "Mass Political Attitudes and the Survey Response." *American Political Science Review* 69: 1218–1231.

Adams, James F., Samuel Merrill III, and Bernard Grofman. 2005. *Unified Theory of Party Competition.* New York: Cambridge University Press.

Aldrich, John H. 1995. *Why Parties? The Origin and Transformation of Political Parties in America.* Chicago: University of Chicago Press.

Alesina, Alberto, and Howard Rosenthal. 1996. "A Theory of Divided Government." *Econometrica* 64: 1311–1342.

Alford, John R., Carolyn L. Funk, and John R. Hibbing. 2005. "Are Political Orientations Genetically Transmitted?" *American Political Science Review* 99: 153–167.

Alvarez, R. Michael. 1998. *Information & Elections.* Ann Arbor: University of Michigan Press. Second edition.

Ansolabehere, Stephen, and Phil Jones. 2006. "Constituents' Policy Perceptions and Approval of their Members of Congress." Typescript, Harvard University.

Ansolabehere, Stephen, Jonathan Rodden, and James M. Snyder. 2008. "The Strength of Issues: Using Multiple Measures to Gauge Preference Stability, Ideological Constraint, and Issue Voting." *American Political Science Review* 102: 215–232.

Ansolabehere, Stephen, James M. Snyder, and Charles Stewart III. 2001. "Candidate Positioning in the U.S. House Elections." *American Journal of Political Science* 45: 136–159.

Bartels, Larry M. 2002. "Beyond the Running Tally: Partisan Bias in Political Perceptions." *Political Behavior* 24 (2): 117–150.

———. 2003. "Democracy with Attitudes." In *Electoral Democracy*, ed. Michael Bruce MacKuen and George Rabinowitz. Ann Arbor: University of Michigan Press.

———. 2006. "What's the Matter with *What's the Matter with Kansas?*" *Quarterly Journal of Political Science* 1: 201–226.

Bartle, John, and Paolo Belluci, eds. 2009. *Political Parties and Partisanship: Social Identity and Individual Attitudes.* London: Routledge.

Berelson, Bernard R., Paul F. Lazarsfeld, and William N. McPhee. 1986. *Voting.* Chicago: University of Chicago Press. Midway Reprint Edition.

Brody, Richard A., and Benjamin I. Page. 1972. "The Assessment of Policy Voting." *American Political Science Review* 66: 979–995.

Bullock, John G. 2009. "Partisan Bias and the Bayesian Ideal in the Study of Public Opinion." *Journal of Politics* 71: 1109–1124.

Campbell, Angus, Philip Converse, Warren Miller, and Donald Stokes. 1960. *The American Voter.* New York: Wiley.

Carmines, Edward G., and James A. Stimson. 1989. *Issue Evolution: Race and the Transformation of American Politics.* Princeton, NJ: Princeton University Press.

Carsey, Thomas M., and Geoffrey C. Layman. 2006. "Changing Sides or Changing Minds? Party Identification and Policy Preferences in the American Electorate." *American Journal of Political Science* 50: 464–477.

Clarke, Harold D., David Sanders, Marianne C. Stewart, and Paul F. Whiteley. 2005. *Political Choice in Britain.* New York: Oxford University Press.

———. 2009. *Performance Politics and the British Voter.* New York: Cambridge University Press.

Converse, Philip E. 1964. "The Nature of Belief Systems in Mass Publics." In *Ideology and Discontent*, ed. David Apter. New York: Free Press.

———. 2000. "Assessing the Capacity of Mass Electorates." *Annual Review of Politics* 3: 331–353.

Cox, Gary W., and Matthew D. McCubbins. 1993. *Legislative Leviathan: Party Government in the House.* Berkeley: University of California Press.

———. 2005. *Setting the Agenda: Responsible Party Government in the U.S. House of Representatives.* New York: Cambridge University Press.

———. 2006. *Legislative Leviathan: Party Government in the House*, 2nd ed. Berkeley: University of California Press.

Cronbach, Lee J., and Paul E. Meehl. 1955. "Construct Validity in Psychological Tests." *Psychological Bulletin* 52: 281–302.

Dawes, Christopher T., and James H. Fowler. 2009. "Partisanship, Voting, and the Dopamine D2 Receptor Gene." *Journal of Politics* 71: 1157–1171.

Delli Carpini, Michael X., and Scott Keeter. 1996. *What Americans Know About Politics and Why It Matters.* New Haven, CT: Yale University Press.

Dennis, J. Michael, and Rick Li. 2005. "Results from a Knowledge Networks' Question Wording Experiment for Political Party Identification." Unpublished research memo.

DiMaggio, Paul, John Evans, and Bethany Bryson. 1996. "Have Americans' Social Attitudes Become More Polarized?" *American Journal of Sociology* 102: 690–755.

Downs, Anthony 1957. *An Economic Theory of Democracy.* New York: Harper & Row.

Elster, Jon. 2007. *Explaining Social Behavior. More Nuts and Bolts for the Social Sciences.* Cambridge: Cambridge University Press.

Evans, John H. 2003. "Have Americans Attitudes Become More Polarized? An Update." *Social Science Quarterly* 84: 71–90.

Ferejohn, John. 1986. "Incumbent Performance and Electoral Control." *Public Choice* 50: 5–25.

Fiorina, Morris P. 1981. *Retrospective Voting in American National Elections.* New Haven, CT: Yale University Press.

———. 1988. "The Reagan Years: Turning to the Right or Groping Toward the Middle?" In *The Resurgence of Conservatism in Anglo- American Democracies*, ed. Barry Cooper, Allan Kornberg, and William Mishler. Durham, NC: Duke University Press.

———. 1990. Information and Rationality in Elections. In *Information and Democratic Processes*, ed. John Ferejohn and James Kuklinski, 329–342. Urbana: University of Illinois Press.

———. 1992. *Divided Government*. New York: Macmillan Press.

Fiorina, Morris P., and Samuel J. Abrams. 2008. "Political Polarization in the American Public." *Annual Review of Political Science* 11: 563–588.

———. 2009. *Disconnect: The Breakdown of Representation in American Politics*. Norman: University of Oklahoma Press.

Fiorina, Morris P., with Samuel J. Abrams, and Jeremy C. Pope. 2005. *Culture War? The Myth of a Polarized America*. New York: Pearson Longman.

Fiorina, Morris P., and Matthew Levendusky. 2006. "Disconnected: The Political Class versus the People." In *Red and Blue Nation? Characteristics, Causes and Chronology of America's Polarized Politics*, ed. Pietro Nivola and David Brady, 49–71, 95–111. Washington, DC: Brookings Institution Press and the Hoover Institution.

Gaines, Brian J., James H. Kuklinski, and Paul J. Quirk. 2007. "The Logic of the Survey Experiment Reexamined." *Political Analysis* 15: 1–20.

Gaines, Brian J., James H. Kuklinski, Paul J. Quirk, Buddy Peyton, and Jay Verkuilen. 2007. "Same Facts, Different Interpretations: Partisan Motivation and Opinion on Iraq." *Journal of Politics* 15: 1–21.

Gelman, Andrew, and Gary King. 1993. "Why are American Presidential Elections Campaign Polls so Variable When Votes Are so Predictable?" *British Journal of Political Science* 23(4): 409–451.

Gerber, Alan, and Donald P. Green. 1998. "Rational Learning and Partisan Attitudes." *American Journal of Political Science* 42: 794–818.

Gintis, Herbert. 2009. *The Bounds of Reason*. Princeton, NJ: Princeton University Press.

Green, Donald, Bradley Palmquist, and Eric Schickler. 2002. *Partisan Hearts and Minds*. New Haven, CT: Yale University Press.

———. 2004. "Downs and Two-Party Convergence." *Annual Review of Political Science* 7: 24–46.

Hardin, Russell. 2009. *How Do You Know? The Economics of Ordinary Knowledge*. Princeton, NJ: Princeton University Press.

Hetherington, Marc. 2001. "Resurgent Mass Partisanship: The Role of Elite Polarization." *American Political Science Review* 95: 619–632.

Hetherington, Marc, and Jonathan Weiler. 2009. *Divided We Stand: Polarization, Authoritarianism, and the Contemporary Political Divide*. Cambridge: Cambridge University Press.

Huddy, Leonie. 2001. "From Social to Political Identity: A Critical Examination of Social Identity Theory." *Political Psychology* 22: 127–156.

———. 2002. "Context and Meaning in Social Identity Theory: A Response to Oakes." *Political Psychology* 23: 825–838.

Iyengar, Shanto. 1986. "Wither Political Information?" Presented at the NES Pilot Study Conference, Ann Arbor.

Jackman, Simon, and Paul M. Sniderman. 2002. "The Institutional Organization of Choice Spaces: A Political Conception of Political Psychology." In *Political Psychology*, ed. Kristen Monroe. Mahwah, NJ: Lawrence Erlbaum.

Jacobson, Gary C. 2005. "Polarized Politics and the 2004 Congressional and Presidential Elections." *Political Science Quarterly* 120 (2): 199–218.

———. 2007. *A Divider, Not a Uniter.* New York: Pearson Longman.

Jacoby, William G. 1988. "The Impact of Party Identification on Issue Attitudes." *American Journal of Political Science* 32: 643–661.

———. 1991. "Ideological Identification and Issue Attitudes." *American Journal of Political Science* 35(1): 178–205.

———. 1995. "The Structure of Ideological Thinking in the American Electorate." *American Journal of Political Science* 39: 314–335.

———. 2010. "The American Voter." In *The Oxford Handbook of American Elections and Political Behavior*, ed. Jan E. Leighley. New York: Oxford University Press.

Jessee, Stephen. 2009. "Spatial Voting in the 2004 Presidential Election" *American Journal of Political Science* 103(1): 59–81.

Johnston, Richard. 2006. "Party Identification: Unmoved Mover or Sum of Preferences?" *Annual Review of Political Science* 9: 329–351.

Kam, Cindy D. 2005. "Who Toes the Party Line? Cues, Values, and Individual Differences." *Political Behavior* 27: 163–182.

Karol, David. 2009. *Party Position Change in American Politics: Coalition Management.* New York: Cambridge University Press.

Kedar, Orit. 2009. *Voting for Policy, Not Parties.* New York: Cambridge University Press.

Key, V. O. 1966. *The Responsible Electorate.* New York: Vintage.

Kinder, Donald R. 1998. "Attitude and Action in the Tealm of Politics." In *Handbook of Social Psychology*, 4th edition, ed. D. Gilbert, S. Fiske, and G. Lindzey, 778–867. Boston, MA: McGraw-Hill.

———. 2003. "Belief systems after Converse." In *Electoral Democracy*, ed. Michael MacKuen and George Rabinowitz, 13–47. Ann Arbor: University of Michigan Press.

Kinder, Donald R., and Nathan P. Kalmoe. 2010. "The Nature of Ideological Identification in Mass Publics: Political Consequences." Midwest Political Science Association National Conference, Chicago, IL.

Krehbiel, Keith. 1998. *Pivotal Politics: A Theory of US Lawmaking.* Chicago: University of Chicago Press.

———. 2010. "Testing Proximity versus Directional Voting Using Experiments." *Electoral Studies* 460–471.

Levendusky, Matthew. 2009a. *The Partisan Sort: How Liberals Became Democrats and Conservatives Became Republicans.* Chicago: University of Chicago Press, Chicago Studies in American Politics Series.

———. 2009b. "Clearer Cues, More Consistent Voters: A Benefit of Elite Polarization." *Political Behavior* 32: 111–131.

Lewis-Beck, Michael S., William C. Jacoby, Helmut Norpoth, and Herbert F. Weisburg. 2008. *The American Voter Revisited*. Ann Arbor: University of Michigan Press.

Lippmann, Walter. 1927. *The Phantom Public*. New York: Harcourt & Brace.

Lodge, Milton, and Charles Taber. *The Rationalizing Voter*. New York: Cambridge University Press, forthcoming.

Madison, James. 1787. "Federalist 10." In *The Federalist Papers*, ed. Alexander Hamilton, James Madison, and John Jay. Reprint: New York: Penguin, 1981.

Malhotra, Neil, Jon A. Krosnick, and Randall K. Thomas. 2009. "Optimal Design of Branching Questions to Measure Bipolar Constructs." *Public Opinion Quarterly* 73: 304–324.

McCarty, Nolan, Keith T. Poole, and Howard Rosenthal. 2006. *Polarized America: The Dance of Ideology and Unequal Riches*. Cambridge, MA: MIT Press.

McKelvey, Richard. 1976. "Intransitivities in Multidimensional Voting Models and Some Implications for Agenda Control." *Journal of Economic Theory* 12: 472–482.

Merolla, Jennifer, Laura B. Stephenson, and Elizabeth Zechmeister. 2008. "Can Canadians Take a Hint? The (In)Effectiveness of Party Labels as Information Shortcuts in Canada." *Canadian Journal of Political Science* 1–24.

Miller, Warren E., and J. Merrill Shanks. 1996. *The New American Voter*. Cambridge, MA: Harvard University Press.

Nelson, Thomas E., and Donald R. Kinder. 1996. "Issue Frames and Group-Centrism in American Public Opinion." *Journal of Politics* 58(4): 1055–1078.

Niemi, Richard G., and M. Kent Jennings. 1991. "Issues and Inheritance in the Formation of Party Identification." *American Journal of Political Science* 35: 970–998.

Parfit, Derek. 2011a. *On What Matters: Volume I*. Oxford: Oxford University Press.

———. 2011b. *On What Matters: Volume II*. Oxford: Oxford University Press.

Poole, Keith T., and Howard Rosenthal. 1997. *Congress: A Political-Economic History of Roll Call Voting*. New York: Oxford University Press.

Rabinowitz, George, and Stuart Elaine Macdonald. 1989. "A Directional Theory of Issue Voting." *American Political Science Review* 83: 93–121.

Rahn, Wendy M. 1993. "The Role of Partisan Stereotypes in Information Processing about Political Candidates. *American Journal of Political Science* 37: 472–496.

Shepsle, Kenneth. 1979. "Institutional Arrangements and Equilibrium in Multidimensional Voting Models." *American Journal of Political Science* 23: 27–60.

Sniderman, Paul M. 2011. "The Logic and Design of the Survey Experiment: An Autobiography of a Methodological Innovation." In *Cambridge Handbook of Experimental Political Science*, ed. James M. Druckman, Donald P. Green, James H. Kuklinski, and Arthur Lupia, 102–114. New York: Cambridge University Press.

Sniderman, Paul, James M. Glaser, and Robert Griffin. 1991. "Information and Electoral Choice." In *Reasoning and Choice*, ed. Paul M. Sniderman, Philip E. Tetlock, and Richard A. Brody. Cambridge: Cambridge University Press.

Sniderman, Paul M., Philip E. Tetlock, and Laurel Elms. 2001. "Public Opinion and Democratic Politics: The Problem of Non-attitudes and Social Construction of Political Judgment." In *Citizens and Politics: Perspectives from Political Psychology*, ed. James H. Kuklinski, 254–284. New York: Cambridge University Press.

Snyder, James M. Jr., and Michael M. Ting. 2002. "An Informational Rationale for Political Parties." *American Journal of Political Science* 46(1): 90–110.

Squire, Peverill, and Eric R. Smith. 1988. "The Effect of Partisan Information on Voters in Nonpartisan Elections." *Journal of Politics* 50: 169–179.

Stiglitz, Edward H., and Barry R. Weingast. 2010. "Agenda Control in Congress: Evidence from Cutpoint Estimates and Ideal Point Uncertainty." *Legislative Studies Quarterly* 35: 157–185.

Stimson, James A. 2004. *The Tides of Consent: How Public Opinion Shapes American Politics*. New York: Cambridge University Press.

Stokes, Donald. E. 1966. "Party Loyalty and the Likelihood of Deviating Elections." In *Elections and the Political Order*, ed. Campbell et al. New York: Wiley.

Stonecash, Jeffrey M. 2000. *Class and Party in American Politics*. Boulder, CO: Westview Press.

Taber, Charles S., and Milton Lodge. 2006. "Motivated Skepticism in the Evaluation of Political Beliefs." *American Journal of Political Science* 50: 655–769.

Taylor, A.J.P. 1983. *A Personal History*. London: Hamish Hamilton.

Theriault, Sean M. 2006. "Procedural Polarization in the US Congress." Paper presented at the annual meeting of the Midwest Political Science Association, Chicago, IL.

Tomz, Michael, and Robert P. Van Houweling. 2008. "Candidate Positioning and Voter Choice." *American Political Science Review* 103: 83–98.

———. 2009. "The Electoral Implications of Candidate Ambiguity." *American Political Science Review* 103: 83–98.

Van Houweling, Robert P., and Paul M. Sniderman. 2004. "The Political Logic of a Downsian Space." Paper presented at the Annual Convention of the Midwest Political Science Association.

Zaller, John. 1992. *The Nature and Origins of Mass Opinion*. Cambridge, UK: Cambridge University Press.

Index